how to build OUTDOOR FIREPLACES and FURNITURE

LARRY EISINGER • EDITOR-IN-CHIEF

THE DO-IT-YOURSELF SERIES

arco publishing co., inc.

NEW YORK CITY 17, NEW YORK

the contents:

the contributors:

HERE IS the complete book for outdoor living. It covers every phase of gracious entertaining in the great out-of-doors. You'll find detailed plans and instructions for building all kinds of attractive, easily-constructed lawn furniture. There are also plans and drawings for the building of many types of barbecues . . . from the simplest, inexpensive model to the deluxe variety. A special section is devoted to excellent, easy-to-make barbecue recipes, the kind that make outdoor eating a real pleasure. And there's an up-to-date survey of all the latest products in the ever-growing field of outdoor living.

OUR FURNITURE and barbecues were built by some of the nation's finest "how-to" writers-designers: David X. Manners, Louis Hochman, Darrell Huff, Paul Corey, and Bill Baker. Mr. Baker, for example, is one of the nation's leading furniture designers. We have previously published two of his books, "Furniture You Can Build" and "Children's Furniture You Can Build."

OUR RECIPE SECTION was compiled by Hyla O'Connor, nationally-known culinary authority. From her vast store of good things to eat, she has come up with many delicious, easy-to prepare recipes for your barbecue parties.

OUR SURVEY of the newest products for outdoor living was made by Griffith Borgeson, well-known authority in this field. His photographic report provides a good look at the barbecue supplies you'll find at local stores.

Dan Blue Editor,

Printed in U. S. A.

MODERN STONE BARBECUE

This easy-to-build fireplace makes a fine family project

By Ralph Mattison

YOUR first step in building this modern stone barbecue will be to determine the right location. Pick a spot accessible to the eating and relaxing area, secluded, and favorable to prevailing winds. It might be advisable to check your local building code regarding any possible restrictions.

The barbecue shown here was built just a few steps from a flagstone terrace bordering on an irregularly-shaped fish pond. The spot chosen was hilly, and the fireplace was set right into the hill.

Use the whole family to dig out the foundation area, as we did. That way they'll know they had a part in the building.

With the digging completed, make a form of wood boards 2x8 inches. The form should measure three feet wide, eight feet long. Be sure this form is absolutely level, and tampered down into the dirt. Then mix and pour concrete into this form to the full length of eight feet. This will give a foundation more than adequate for the purpose. For additional strength, you can put in a few iron reinforcing rods. Keep the footing wet and in the curing process for about a week.

The base, which contains storage and cooking areas, is red face brick. The spacious working areas on top of the storage compartments are blue stone slabs. The chimney is beautiful gray Crab Orchard

FIRST STEP is to choose location, mark it off with string, dig bed for concrete base. Be sure sides and floor are kept level.

WOODEN FORM is put in place. Since location is a hillside, slope was used to nestle rear of fireplace. Form must be level.

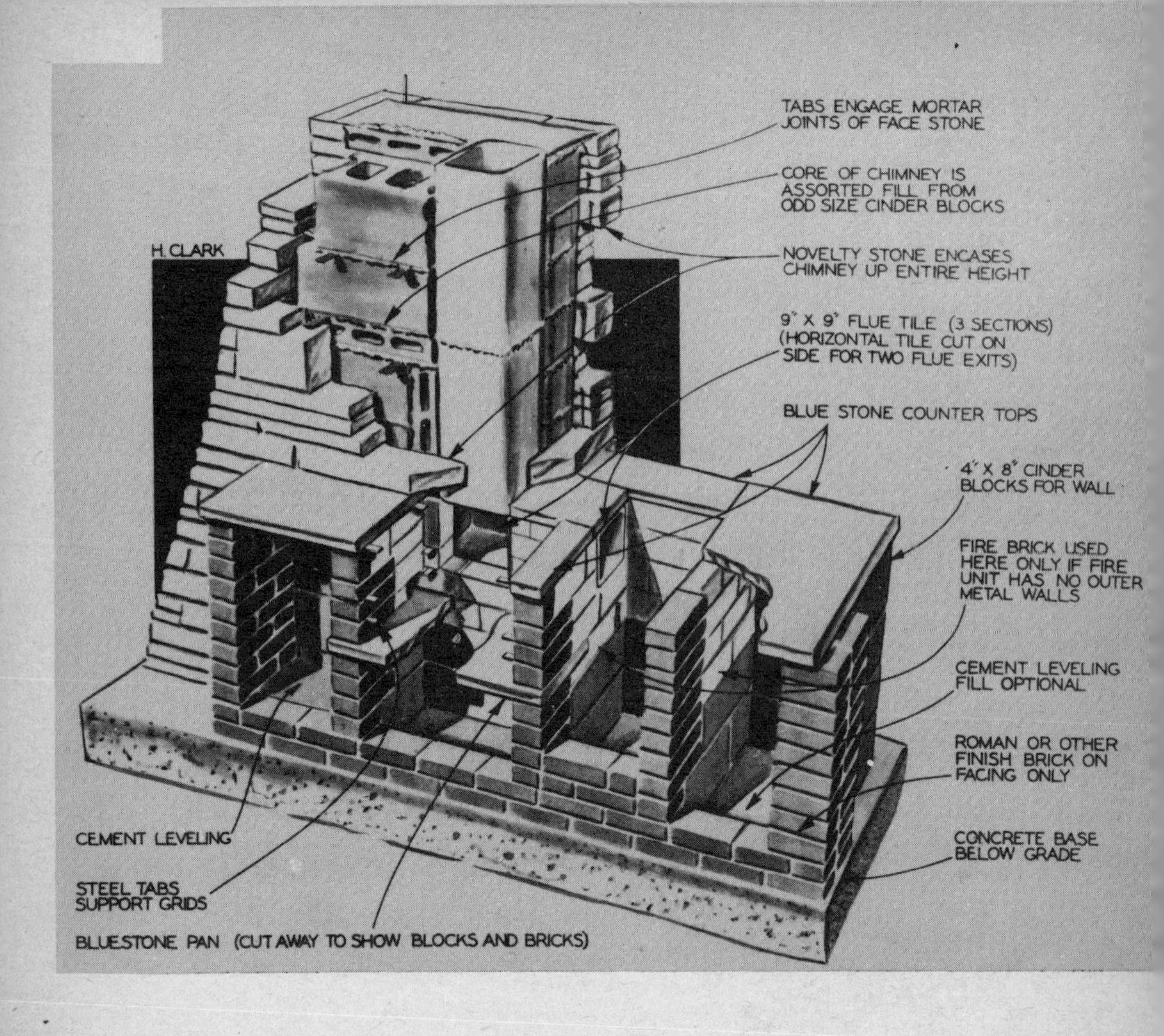

AFTER CONCRETE has "cured" for a week, begin to set up blocks at rear, and red facing brick, as shown. Before tying these permanently together with mortar, it's wise to see if pieces fit properly.

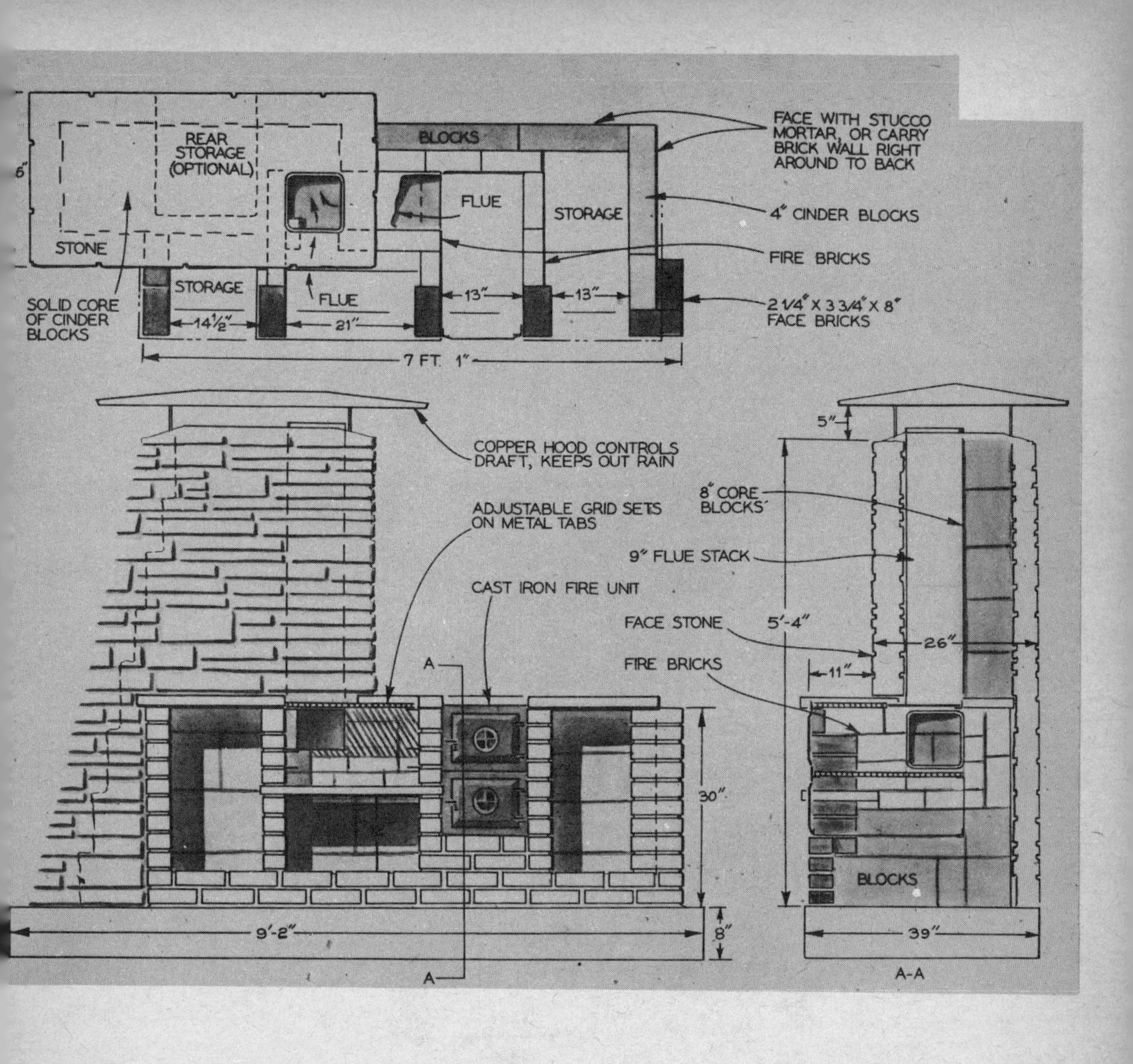

WHEN YOU are sure each unit of design fits into proper place, take away top bricks and apply mortar to lower layers. Then build up layer by layer as planned in your earlier game of "block building."

ON THE WAY toward completion, fireplace now has all basic unit-areas permanently defined. Before mortared joints are dry, however, check to be sure grills, shelves and firebox fit the areas allotted for them.

NEXT STAGE toward completion is building up the walls in front of barbecue, then the walls along the sides. Build both groups up to their full height. Do neat and careful job.

THIS PHOTO shows how bluestone shelf is placed. First lay bricks up to required height (4 bricks high over bottom 2-brick-layers) then place shelf and set permanently with mortar. Add four bricks on top.

TAKING SHAPE, fireplace now has flue and cinder block interior of chimney in place. Drawing on page 6 shows exact stage of construction at this point. Note cinder block in rear wall of the barbecue.

READY FOR the chimney facing of Crab Orchard stone, one work area of bluestone is now already set. The Crab Orchard stone will be built up around the cinder block and flue tiles.

CHIMNEY FACING is easy to place. Varying shapes and colors of stones offer many possibilities in design. As you progress in this work, you'll probably become fancier and fancier, do a spectacular job.

NEARING job's end, second bluestone work table is laid on right side of fireplace and along the right rear.

FINAL touch is the copper hood which serves to keep rain out of the cooking units, adds a handsome atmosphere.

COMPLETED fireplace sets well with surroundings of foliage in back yard. A few flagstones in front always help.

stone, which is built up around the cinder block and flue tiles. The design of this fireplace is so flexible that many other materials might easily be used.

The firebox is a ready-made unit, fitted with lift-out lids and grates. Manufactured by the Majestic Company, this unit has a regular grate in front. The rear section has a plate for frying.

When starting to build this barbecue, set your first layer of blocks, bricks, fireplace unit and grates into position atop your chosen footing area before pouring concrete. This precaution makes doubly certain that everything is going to fit.

After the concrete facing is laid, you can start building. Outside of your facing, around the fireplace unit and open grill, use fire brick. And don't forget to install hangers for the grates around the grill while laying the fire brick. It's very easy to forget this.

In laying and cutting the Crab Orchard stone you'll have a lot of fun and more than likely find yourself getting a bit fancy toward the top, doing things you wouldn't have dreamed of when you began. The stone lends itself nicely to abstract design as photos here show. •

MATERIALS NEEDED:

- 24 8x8x16-inch cinder blocks
- 60 4x8x16-inch cinder blocks for chimney, back and side of base
- 3 sections 8x8x24-inch flue tiles for chimney
- 150 2x4x8-inch red face bricks for base
- 50 2x4x8-inch fire bricks for use around cooking units
- 25 corrugated wall ties for securing Crab Orchard stone to cinder block
- 9 bags Portland cement footing, base and chimney
- 1 ton Crab Orchard stone chimney facing
- 1 yard sand 1 yard gravel
- 1 Majestic fireplace unit
- 2 Majestic grates
- 8 hangers for grates in open grill
- 1 sheet copper, angle iron, bolts and bolt sticks for hood

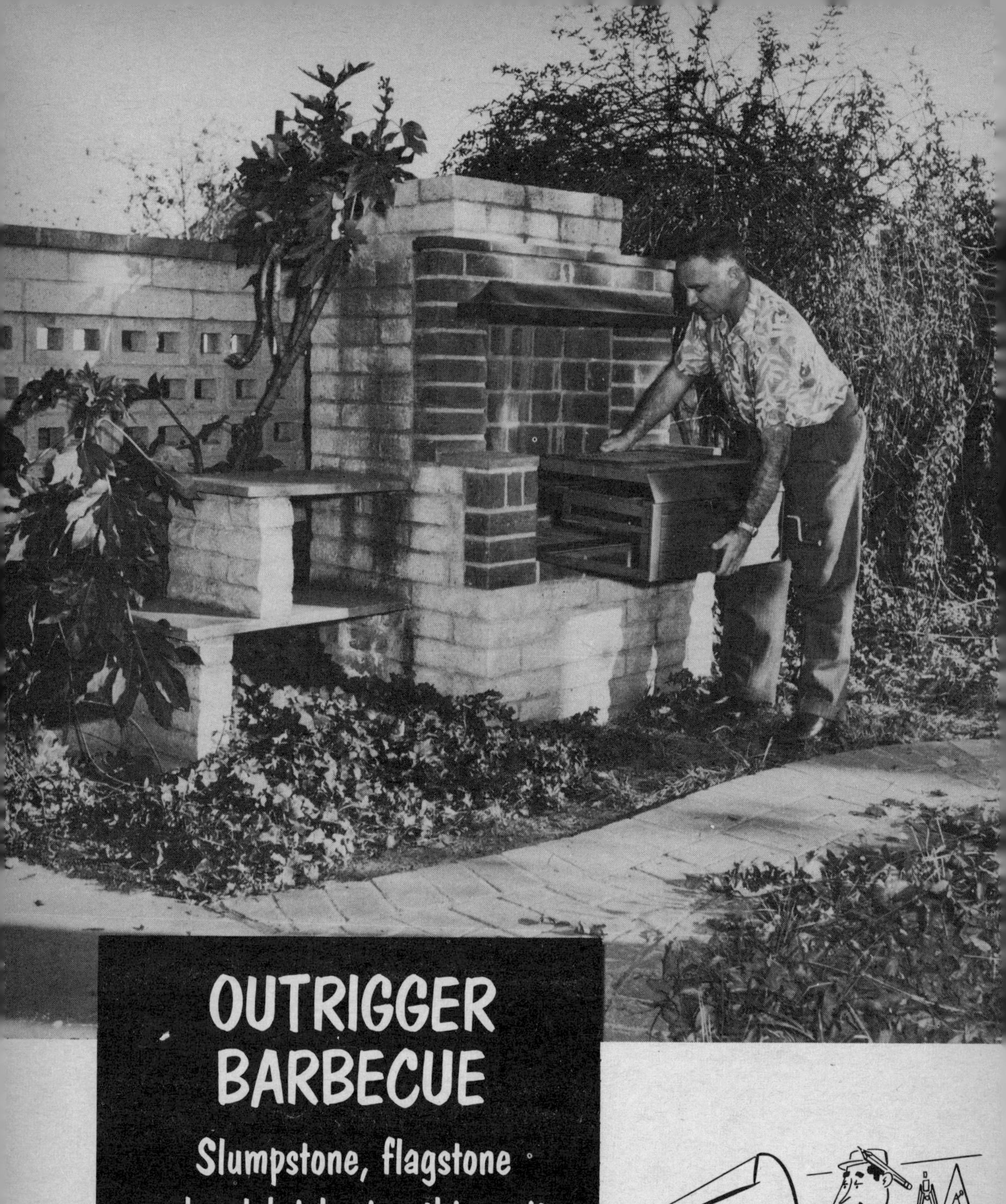

OUTRIGGER BARBECUE

Slumpstone, flagstone and red brick give this unit a rustic appearance

By Louis Hochman

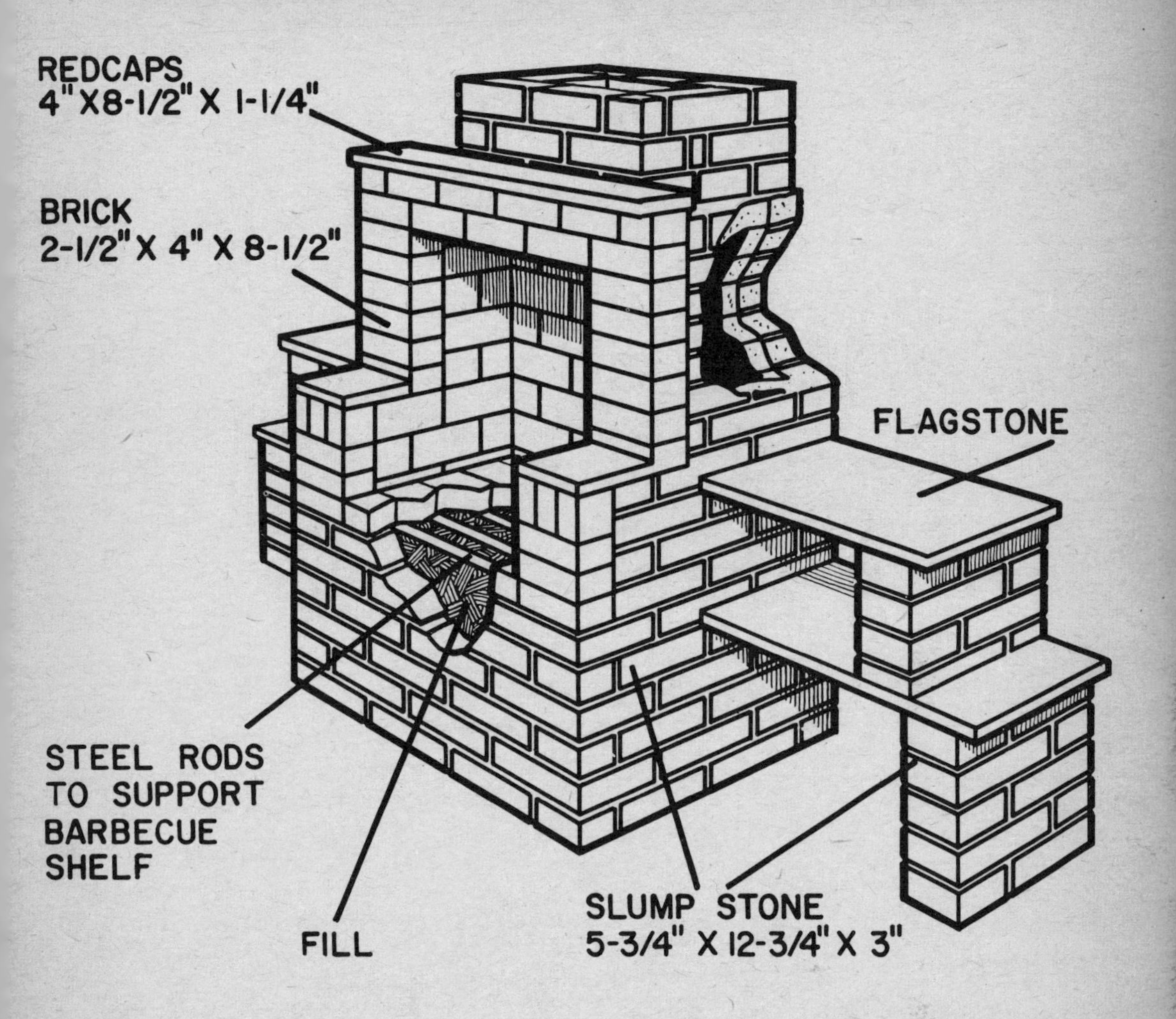

FOR simplicity of construction and beauty of design, the outrigger barbecue made by Outdoor Sales and Construction Co., of Sherman Oaks, California, is a sure bet.

Through the use of attractive slumpstone, flagstone and red brick, it achieves a rustic quality that sets it apart from the average commercial type barbecue, and makes it ideal for informal garden settings.

Basically, the Outrigger consists of a single unit which accommodates a 27½-inch Albert Control-A-Fire Grill or a 28-inch wide Burr Fireplace Adjustafire unit. Jutting out from the sides of this main barbecue unit, are a series of flagstone table shelves which provide plenty of working space while cooking and can hold decorated potted plants, pottery, or ceramics when not in use.

The barbecue is mainly built of 5¾x12¾x3-inch slumpstone, a variety of concrete block that has a rough-hewn texture somewhat like field stone. The base is built six courses high and should measure 45 inches across the front by 2 feet 8 inches along the side. Across the top of the sixth course, lay a series of steel reinforcing rods to support the bricks of the firebox floor. The rods should be ½ inch round by 3 feet 9 inches long.

Next, lay a course of bricks across the front of the unit, then build the sides and back up with four additional slumpstone courses. The brick floor of the firebox section should then be laid across the steel

rods. Line the inside walls with brick, too, as you build up the slumpstone course. After the tenth course of slumpstone, the sides of the barbecue narrow down abruptly from the base dimension of two feet by 8 inches to a continuing width of 32½ inches. This leaves two small 8½x8¼-inch ledges on each side of the barbecue opening which are then topped off with red caps.

Face With Brick

From the sixth course up, the front of the barbecue is faced with brick, as shown. The pit opening should be from 28½ to 29 inches wide to accommodate the grill unit. Its depth should be 21¾ inches and lined on the inside with bricks up the back as shown in diagram. Use a 3x3-inch, 30-inch long angle iron or lintel across the top of the opening to support the top rows of bricks. Trim the top of the bricks along the front of the chimney with a row of 4x8½x1¼-inch red caps.

Slumpstone is used for the chimney and a pair of steel rods should be bridged across the top to support the front row of slumpstones. Support for the sides of the

WING TABLES are cut from inch-thick flagstone, the top table measuring 18x24, the lower 18x32 inches.

THIS VIEW of outrigger barbecue shows completed barbecue without the fireplace unit set in its place.

COMPLETED BARBECUE looks like this, uses Albert Control-A-Fire Grill or Burr Fireplace Adjustafire.

chimney is provided by tapering the brick lining on the inside wall inward at the top.

The wing tables are cut from inch-thick flagstone, the top tables measuring 18x24 inches and the lower ones, 18x32 inches. Steel pegs to support the tables where they contact the barbecue should project from the masonry between the fifth and sixth courses and the ninth and tenth courses on each side of the unit. These should be inserted when those courses are laid. The outer extremities of the tables are supported on legs of slumpstone as shown, stacking the stones five high under the lower table and four high between the lower and upper table. Allow two inches overhang past the slumpstone supports, and mortar the joints where the flagstone tables butt up against the barbecue unit proper.

The barbecue should be set on a six-inch thick concrete foundation and if this foundation does not extend to the table supports, provide concrete footings for the slumpstone legs by digging six-inch deep, 6x12-inch trenches under each support and filling these with concrete. •

RUSTIC QUALITY of barbecue sets it apart from average commercial type, makes it ideal for garden.

DIAGRAMS BELOW give all the necessary measurements needed to build the outrigger barbecue. Study them carefully, consult them from time to time. Result will be a barbecue of which you can be proud.

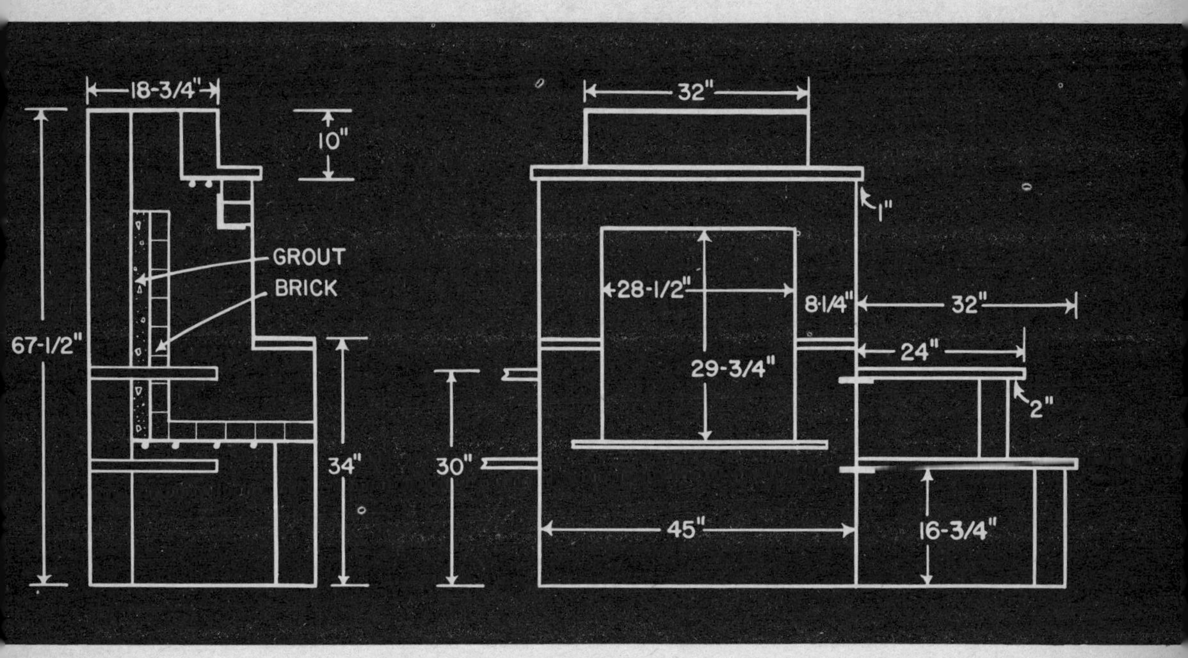

HAPPY HOLIDAY BARBECUE

This unit serves as a backyard divider as well as a barbecue

By Louis Hochman

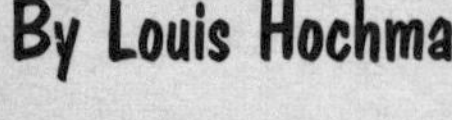

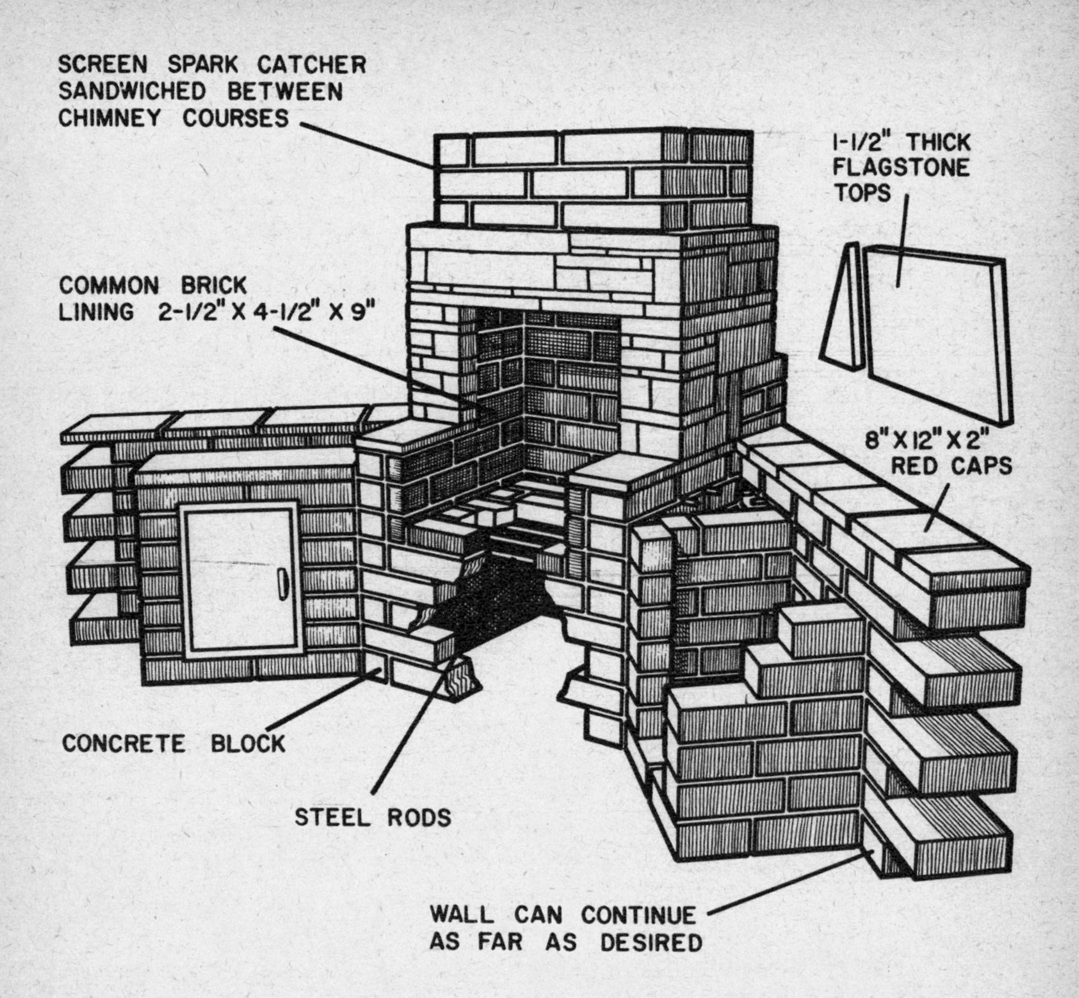

HERE is a colorful barbecue that combines stained concrete blocks with rustic flagstone and firebrick to make outdoor picnicking a holiday event. The unit, built by California Patios of Sherman Oaks, Cal., sets diagonally into a corner of the patio and is an integral part of the concrete block wall that backs it. In fact, the wall forms the back of the barbecue and can end with the barbecue itself, or continue on for any desired distance to divide the patio or yard from the neighboring grounds.

In order to get the decorative staggered pattern in the concrete block construction, blocks of three varying lengths (6, 8, and 12 inches respectively) are used. These are stained in various colors with Kemiko concrete stain to produce the desired varicolored effect. In laying the courses, select the variety of lengths for each course that will work out to the even length required. Make this selection before mortaring any of the blocks in place, then line them up to form the most pleasing pattern for staggered sizes and color, and mortar them into place in that order. Each following course should be selected to contrast with the previous course.

The main section of the barbecue is designed to take a 28-inch wide Albert Control-A-Fire Grill or the Allied Mfg. Co. grill shown in photos. This unit fits snugly into the 28½-inch wide cooking chamber. The base of the main section is made of concrete block eight courses high on the sides, and five courses high in the front. Across the tops of the fifth course, lay a series of parallel ⅜-inch round, 40-inch long steel reinforcing rods to support the bed of firebrick to be laid over them. Space the rods approximately three inches apart. The cavity under this firebox can be filled with dirt if desired.

Add three more courses up the sides and back above the steel rods, then set the fire

FIREPLACE UNIT in barbecue is made by the Allied Manufacturing Company. It fits into 28½-inch cooking chamber.

bricks on the rods, using plenty of mortar to bond them to the rods and each other. Pave this firebox floor with firebricks to a depth of 21½ inches; then set the rear courses vertically to form the back wall of the firebox. The inside side walls should also be lined with firebrick as shown in diagrams. If the rear wall of the barbecue unit is never seen, it can be built with concrete block. Otherwise, flagstone rock should be used above the eighth course of concrete block. From the eighth course on, the sides and front of the barbecue unit are built with flagstone rock, selecting sizes and strips to form the most pleasing design and texture. The two ledges that flank the grill unit are topped with 8½x12-inch rectangles of inch-thick flagstone.

The flagstone portion of the walls should extend to a height of 5 feet 1½ inches from

MATERIALS NEEDED:

- 500 lbs. flagstone rock
- 65 fire bricks (8½x4x2½)
- 25 concrete blocks (6x4x12)
- 25 concrete blocks (6x4x8)
- 4 concrete blocks (6x4x6)
- 10 red caps (2x8x12)
- 170 concrete blocks (6x4x16)
- 15 concrete blocks (6x4x14)
- 2 Flagstone tops, 20x30x1-inch thick
- 1 Flagstone top, 18x20-inch cut in half diagonally
- 2 Flagstone tops, 8½x12-inch
- 2 Steel reinforcing rods, ⅜-inch round by 42-inch long
- 5 Steel reinforcing rods, ⅜-inch round by 40-inch long
- 1 3x3 angle iron, 40-inch long
- 1 Spark arrestor 12x36-inch, ½-inch mesh 12 gauge
- 2 14x20-inch Burr Steel Doors
- 1 28-inch wide Albert Control-A-Fire Grill unit
- 1 Hood 30-inch wide at top flanging out to 38-inch
- 1 ton plaster sand
- ½ ton pea gravel (For foundation mix)
- 3 sacks plastic cement

For the mortar, mix 5 parts sand to 1 part cement.

For the Foundation, mix 3 parts sand to 4 parts gravel and 1 part cement.

the ground, at which point the chimney section begins. For this section, we go back to concrete block, building it three courses high and sandwiching a 20x36-inch rectangle of 12-gauge, ½-inch wire mesh between the second and third course, as shown in diagram. This wire mesh serves as the spark catcher. Because the chimney has narrower dimensions than the main unit, two steel rods, ⅜ inch round by 42 inches long, must be bridged across the top opening to form a support for the front row of blocks used in the chimney.

Extending at an angle of 45 degrees on each side of this main unit are two storage compartments topped with flagstone tabletops which provide generous work surfaces. Start by laying out the back walls of unstained concrete block, setting these walls at 45-degree angles to the sides of the barbecue unit. These walls form the backs of the storage compartments and should be eight courses high, topped with 8x12x2-inch red caps. The storage units are then built up against this back wall, making them 28 inches wide at the front and seven courses high. Because of the difficulty of cutting the flagstone top in one piece, it is better to do it in two pieces, one piece measuring 20x30 inches and the other a triangle measuring 18x20 inches on its right angle sides. A simple way is to take an 18x20 inch rectangle of flagstone and cut it diagonally in half to make the two triangles needed on each side of the barbecue.

In the front of the storage units, leave 14x20 inch masonry openings as shown to accommodate 14x20 inch Burr steel doors.

The concrete foundation for the main unit should be at least six inches thick. •

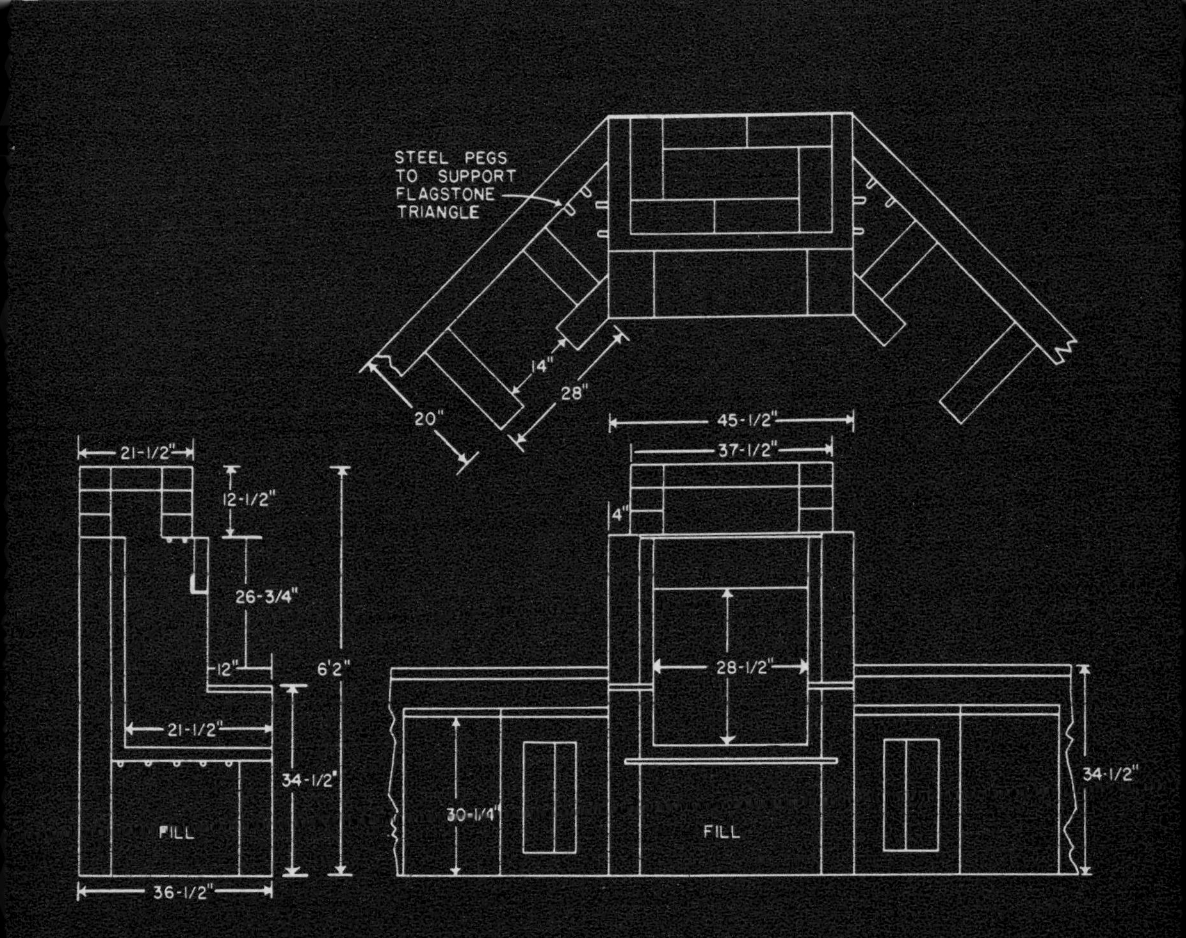

BLOCK-AND-BRICK BARBECUE

This combination makes for easy construction and attractive appearance

By David X. Manners

IF YOU want to build a barbecue, but don't relish the effort involved, use block in its construction. Every block is the equivalent of about a dozen bricks. Straight block construction may not be as attractive as all-brick construction, but in combination with brick it is indeed practical and handsome. The 42 blocks used in the construction can readily be placed in a couple of hours. It would take more than a day to lay the 500 bricks that otherwise would be required.

Preferably, locate the barbecue so it faces in the direction of prevailing winds. You'll find it burns better, and that the draft will carry the smoke produced by ignited drippings away from the cooking area.

Drive in stakes to mark the four corners of the subbase (A), which measures 58x76 inches. Then string a line from stake to stake to outline the rectangle. Use a rafter square to make sure all corners of the rectangle are right angles. If you don't have a rafter square, measure the diagonals of the area you have laid out. They should be equal in length. If the diagonals are not equal, the layout is lopsided. True up the corners so that the diagonals are equal.

Dig out the area to a depth of 8 to 10 inches and backfill to within 3½ inches of the top with crushed rock, cinders or gravel. This provides good drainage under the slab and minimizes the chances of frost damage. With a tamper or garden roller, compact the fill and be sure it is level. Wetting down the fill will aid in compaction, and will also prevent the fill from sucking water from the concrete that's to be poured on it.

Form for Barbecue

Make a form for the concrete slab (B) out of 2x4's, using two nails at each corner. If you don't drive the nails all the way in, they'll be easier to pull out when you remove the form after the concrete has set. Brace the form now by driving in foot-long stakes along its perimeter. Inside measurement of the form should be 54x72 inches. Use a spirit level to make sure each of the four sides of the form is level. Then check the level across the form from side to side and from front to back.

Approximately 8 cubic feet of concrete will be needed for the 3½-inch slab. Make the concrete of 1 part cement, 2 parts sand and 4 parts gravel or crushed stone. In most areas you can get sand and gravel already mixed in proper proportion. Allowing for waste, you'll need approximately two sacks of cement ($1.50 per) and 12

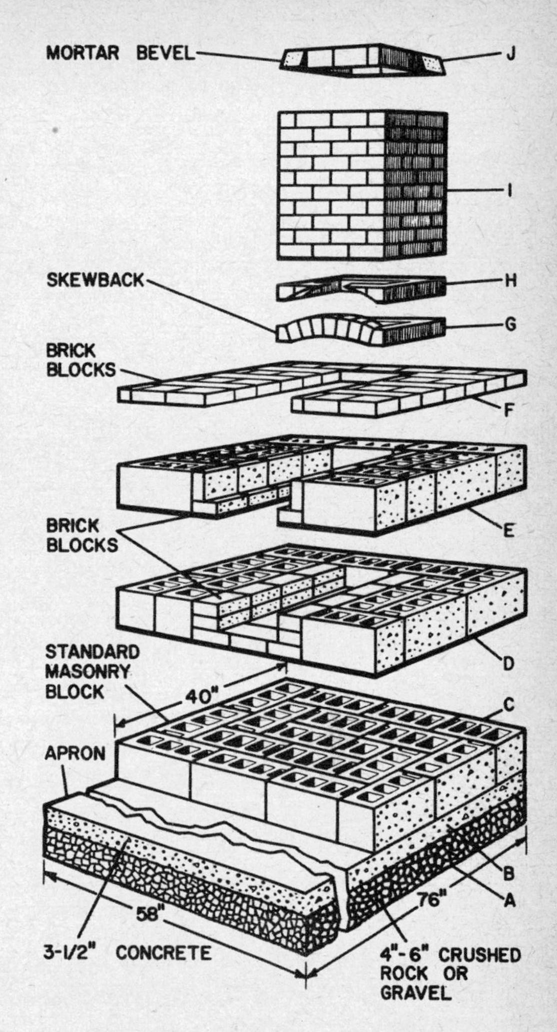

CUT MASONRY BLOCKS with a chisel, or chop apart with the edged end of bricklayer's hammer.

cubic feet of sand-and-gravel mix ($2.75 will buy a half yard). Mix dry ingredients thoroughly before adding water, and use no more than five gallons to a sack of cement. If you use Sakrete gravel mix for the job, you'll need about twelve of the 90-lb. sacks (about $1.25 per).

Pour the concrete, leveling it off even with the top of the form by using a straight-edged board. When the concrete has begun to set fairly stiff (probably an hour or two), use a wood float to smooth off the surface of apron to a final finish, but keep the slab under the barbecue proper rough. This will insure a good bond with the blocks above. Cure the slab by keeping it moist for at least 48 hours.

Building Barbecue

You can start on the barbecue structure as soon as the concrete is hard enough to bear weight. The mortar used in this construction is 1 part mortar cement and 3 parts sand. Thoroughly mix these two ingredients before adding just enough water to make a workable blend. A batch made by mixing three shovels of cement and nine of sand is the most you should mix at one time, for mortar should be used up within about half an hour after preparation. One sack of cement will provide enough mortar for laying 250 bricks, so you can figure on about 1½ sacks for the entire block-and-brick operation.

Experimentally, place the first course of blocks (C) dry to verify fit and arrangement, then remove the blocks, spread a ½-inch layer of mortar on the slab and set the blocks permanently. With a trowel, butter the wing ends of each block with mortar before setting it in place against its neighbor. Use the end of the trowel handle to tap the block level. A rafter square is handy for squaring corners.

The second course (D) of the barbecue includes solid masonry blocks, often called brick blocks. Used here as the ashpit base, they cover the voids of the blocks in the course below. If desired, fire brick or the same kind of face brick that is to be used for the chimney can be substituted.

Because bricks and brick blocks may vary in size, some trimming may be necessary to achieve the pattern shown. In construction of the barbecue as illustrated blocks adjacent to the ashpit lining were trimmed. Regular masonry blocks are readily cut with a chisel, brick-set, or with the edged end of a bricklayer's hammer. Cut or chop the block all the way around, but be careful of flying chips. Wearing of protective goggles may be advisable.

Compact the joints of each course as it is completed, using either a regular jointing tool, a piece of ¾-inch pipe, or a dowel. Compact the vertical joints, then the horizontal.

Brick blocks for the ashpit base are laid parallel to the front of the barbecue, and with unbroken joints. The sides of the pit are built up with two courses of brick blocks laid at right angles to the base. Mortar joints may be kept thin here, if required —$\frac{1}{16}$ inch being sufficient.

With this course (D) completed, begin placement of the next course (E). Note

IF CAPPING COURSE on base doesn't fit exactly, finish off attractively with mortar bevel, as shown.

FIRE IS BUILT on lower grate. Arch eliminates the need for a supporting lintel across the opening.

that the second of the two courses of brick for the ashpit walls is set on edge. As you proceed, constantly use the spirit level not only to verify that each course is level, but that the vertical faces are plumb. If you do not have a level, a straight-edged board may help in keeping block faces in line. A plumb bob or a weighted string will serve in determining vertical alignments.

Brick blocks are also used for the capping course (F). Place them as shown in the diagram. Do not worry about the blocks covering the area exactly. The rear edge, or the side edges, can be beveled with mortar. This capping course serves as a work area and a place on which to rest cooking equipment. The cooking grill rests on the cap's inside edges. The fire grate is the same size as the cooking grill (18x24 incnes), but it is turned so that its short side is forward. It rests on the brick blocks forming the sides of the ashpit (D).

Dampen Bricks

A good quality face brick is desirable for the chimney, but common brick or even used brick will serve. Approximately 230 standard size brick are needed (4c each and up). Dampen the brick before laying them. Dry bricks will rob the mortar of its moisture and make it crumble.

The first chimney course (G) includes an arch. The arch, which adds distinction to the design, is simple to construct and is stronger than a metal lintel. It does, however, require a wooden support until it is set. Cut a board to correspond to the curve of the arch (a 20-inch radius), and prop it in place by any improvised means. Make the support easy to remove when the arch has set.

The seven bricks comprising the arch proper are all half bricks. Note the angle cut of the "skewback" bricks on either side of the arch. Cutting these bricks at an angle is important to the proper construction of the arch. Also note the trimming of bricks in the next course (H). This trimming, done with chisel or brick-set, levels off the construction thus far and puts everything back on an even keel.

Ten courses of brick (I) bring the chimney up to a proper level for the finishing course (J). Bricks in the finishing course are set on their side, rather than flat. This permits a mortar bevel, which is not only attractive, but also helps shed water and prevents moisture penetration of the brick joints below.

The top of the chimney should be at least at eye level, never below it. If you are well over six feet and plan to do the chefing, you may find it desirable to add an extra course or two of brick before placing the capping course.

Do not build a fire in the barbecue for two weeks. Break it in carefully then with a small fire that's kept burning for several hours. It's wise to repeat this break-in every spring. In the winter, metal parts are easily removable for storage. Always leave cooking grease on the grill until just before its next use. It keeps the grill from rusting between times.

Keep these pointers in mind as you build this barbecue. •

LIST BELOW gives the materials needed to build barbecue. Use of masonry blocks saves time, effort.

CAP COURSE on chimney is made by setting the bricks on edge, then filling between with mortar.

FIREPLACE UNIT (Albert Control-A-Grill) fits into barbecue in area shown in these two photographs.

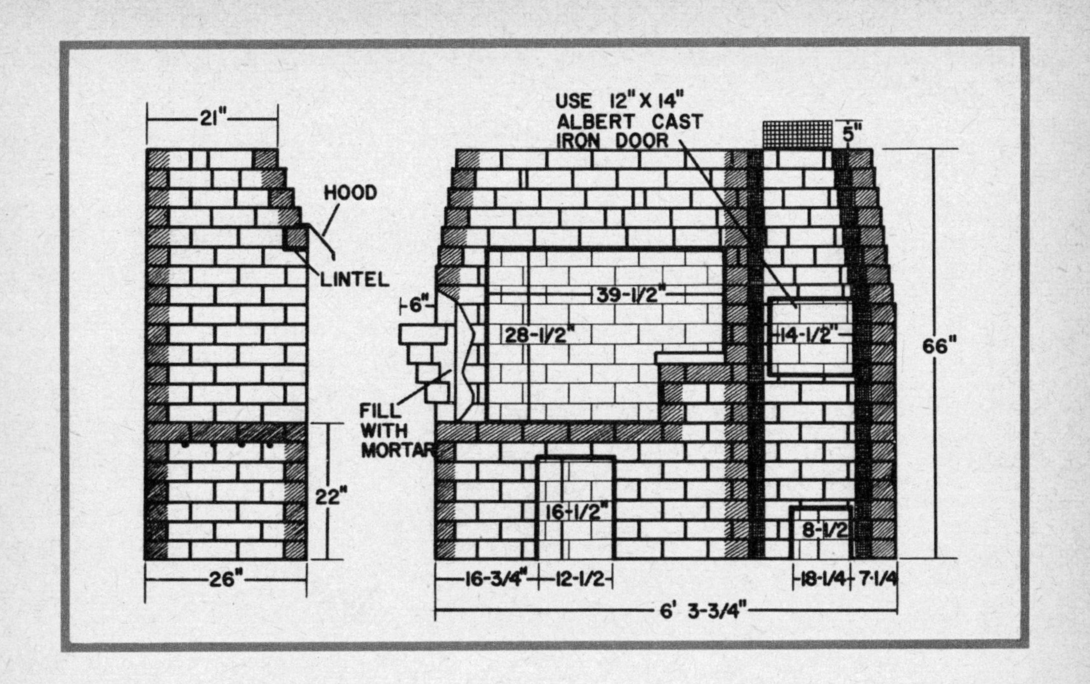

DOUBLE-DUTY BARBECUE

It contains a brick barbecue and an incinerator in one compact unit

By Louis Hochman

CLEANING up after a paper-plate outdoor barbecue party is a cinch with this double-purpose brick barbecue which combines both a barbecue and an incinerator in one compact decorative unit. Designed and built by Outdoor Sales and Construction Co. of Sherman Oaks, Calif., the barbecue is made entirely of brick, both common and firebrick and will accommodate a 17½-inch wide Albert Control-A-Grill barbecue unit. One of the attractive features of the unit is its unique cooking chamber which is shaped like an inverted "L" to provide an 11-inch work shelf alongside and on a level with the barbecue grill. This shelf is topped with 3½x11½x1½-inch red cap, and can also serve as a warming shelf to keep bread and other foods close to the warmth of the charcoal fire.

An inside 5¼-inch thick wall divides the unit into two separate chambers, allowing for the incinerator section on the right. This trash burning section should be lined with an inner wall of firebrick, to provide sufficient heat insulation. The grate for the incinerator is made by bridging a series of parallel ½-inch round 20-inch long steel rods across the outer and inner walls at a height approximately 12 inches from the

INCINERATOR in barbecue should be lined with inner wall of firebrick to provide sufficient heat insulation.

ground. The ends of these steel rods are embedded into the mortar between the brick courses.

Steel rods are also installed in a similar manner across the sixth course of bricks on the other side to support the firebox floor of the cooking chamber, as shown in diagram. Butter each brick well with mortar before laying it on the rod shelf so that it will bond to the rods and form a solid base.

The space under the cooking chamber serves as a storage bin for fuel and tools. Leave a 12½x16½-inch masonry opening as shown, to accommodate a 12x16 Albert Steel door. To the right of this door in the incinerator section, leave a masonry opening of 8¼x10¼ inches for an 8x10 Albert Steel door. This is the cleanout section for removal of ashes from the incinerator.

The opening for the incinerator door should begin with the ninth course of bricks, and should measure 14½ inches wide by 12½ inches high. This opening will take a 12x14 cast iron Albert door.

To support the bricks across the top of the barbecue pit opening, mortar a 4-foot long, 4x4-inch angle iron, or lintel, across the 16th course of bricks as shown in diagram. The bricks can then be laid directly on this lintel to bridge the opening.

On the side of the structure near the barbecue, a small decorative brick shelf is built out as shown to serve either as a

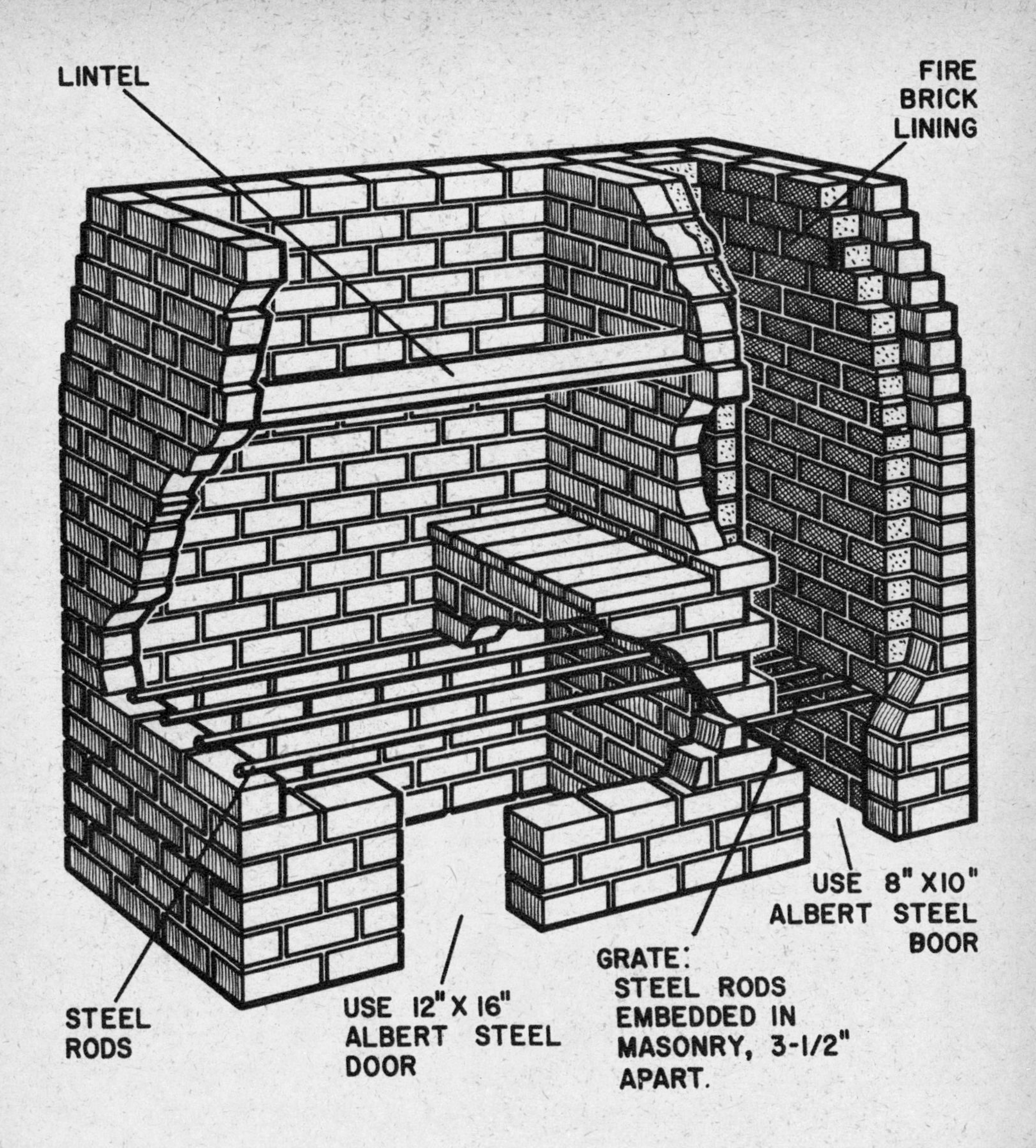

flower pot holder or as a place to lay the cooking utensils down while working. Make this by letting one of the brick in the ninth course jut out about 1 inch from the surface of the side wall. The brick directly above this one can jut out about an inch further, and the one above this can jut out its full 4-inch width. These staggered bricks form the bracket support for the final two bricks which are laid on them parallel to each other and at right angles to the wall, as shown. The gap left on the inside surface of the wall where the bricks jut out, should then be filled with mortar as the inner layer of bricks are added to for the double thickness side wall.

The top of the unit tapers slightly to angle the lines inward toward the chimney end. To achieve this effect, step the bricks inward toward the top, offsetting each course on the barbecue side about ¾ inch, and on the incinerator side about ½ inch. Start off-setting on the barbecue side with the 16th course, and on the incinerator side with the 14th course. The front should also be tapered inward at the top in the same manner, starting with the 18th course.

On the incinerator side, allow an 8x8½-inch chimney opening in the top and cover this with a 5-inch high box-shaped spark catcher made of 12 gauge, ½-inch wire mesh. Allow the finished barbecue to cure for two weeks, sprinkling it daily for the first week, before using it. •

SMALL BLOCK BARBECUE

It costs less than $10 to build, will give years of satisfaction

By David X. Manners

HERE'S a barbecue you can build in three hours and which will give satisfaction and pleasure for many years. The cost is well under $10.

A foundation slab is important in a barbecue. It ties the entire structure together so that, like a boat, it can float undamaged over any ground swells caused by frost or earth movement. But you needn't do the heavy work of pouring a concrete foundation for this barbecue. Make a matte of reinforced brick instead.

On a firm, well-drained site, dig out an area measuring 38x40 inches to a depth of six inches. Level off the bottom of the excavation and tamp it well. Place bricks in a basket pattern—three this way, three that—to fill the area. Mix a mortar batch of one part mortar cement, three parts sand.

Then, after thoroughly blending the dry ingredients, add water until the mix has the consistency of mud. With your trowel, shovel the mortar between brick joints to half their depth.

Reinforcing Rod

Cut a 20-foot length of ½-inch reinforcing rod into six lengths measuring 40 inches each. The rod is readily cut with a hacksaw. Make cut halfway through, then break rod apart. Place a rod in each of the cracks that transverses the matte. Fill the cracks with mortar flush with the top.

On a bed of mortar, and two inches in from the rear of the base, place two masonry blocks to form the back of the barbecue, and a block to form each side. With bricks placed flat in a mortar bed, fill in between the blocks and make an apron

UNIT requires only 12 masonry blocks and 68 common bricks. Reinforcing rods serve as both the grate and the grill.

EXCAVATE AREA measuring 38x40 inches to a depth of about six inches. Level and tamp the area.

PLACE DAMP, not wet, bricks on edge in basket-weave pattern—three this way and three that way.

FILL CRACKS to half depth with mortar, place three ½x40-inch reinforcing rods across matte each way.

FILL CRACKS to top with mortar and smooth. No need to wait for setting, go ahead with block work.

PLACE BLOCKS in bed of mortar, two blocks forming rear of unit, a block on each side. Check level.

FILL AREA between blocks and apron with bricks laid flat, joints unbroken. Set grate rods in place.

PLACE SECOND course of blocks, staggering joints. Cut block with brick, cold chisel for half blocks.

PLACE THREE ⅝x27-inch rods across the unit to make the grill, then add the top course of blocks.

FILL CAVITIES of blocks with stones or rubble, or pack in crumpled newspaper within inch of top.

FINISH OFF top of blocks with mortar, leveled smooth, or crowned slightly at the center, as shown.

PUNCH HOLES at intervals in a 15½x15½-inch sheet of heavy metal. Fold over sheet edges.

INSERT SHEET into barbecue. It forms fire pan, rests on the grate bars which were installed earlier.

COMPLETED UNIT looks like this. Barbecue is easy to build, will give excellent service for many years, many barbecues.

in front of them. Lay bricks roman style, that is, with unbroken joints.

Cut six 27-inch lengths of ⅝-inch reinforcing rod. Place three of the rods across the barbecue as a grate before adding the second course of blocks. Atop the second course, add the remaining three bars to form the grill. Now add the third and final course.

Fill in the cavities of the blocks with rubble and mortar and finish smooth. In a 15½x15½-inch square of heavy sheet metal punch holes at two- to three-inch intervals. Edges of sheet may be bent double for reinforcement. Sheet metal pan is supported by grate—and barbecue is ready for use. •

MATERIALS NEEDED:

12 masonry blocks
68 bricks
6 rods ½x40 inches
6 rods ⅝x27 inches
1 bag mortar cement
2½ cu. ft. sand

HANDY ROD GRILLS can be placed on rods, will hold hamburgers, hot dogs, even large steaks.

SMOKE OVEN

It not only smoke-cooks food, but also serves as a barbecue and hot plate

By David X. Manners

FOR centuries the Chinese have practiced smoke oven cooking. Once you've sampled some, you'll understand why. Turkey, shrimp, hamburgers, oysters, duckling, steak, salmon, chops, spareribs, haddock, game, sturgeon, cheese—all have an indescribably delicious flavor when smoke cooked.

Food to be cooked is hung from hooks in the "chimney" where fragrant smoke collects from a hardwood fire built in the firechamber. A damper on the lid covering the chimney is regulated to control the fire and produce the degree of heat desired. An inexpensive oven thermometer hung in the chimney is an accurate temperature guide, but you can follow instinct, if you prefer.

Most meats cook best at about 300 degrees. For a rare steak, do a 3-inch cut for 20 to 30 minutes at 300. Hamburgers and hot dogs are cooked in 5 to 10 minutes at 300. Pork chops are ready after about 45 minutes at 350-degrees. Marinate food before cooking for varying taste.

Since the smoke oven is actually nothing but a barbecue with an oversize chimney, it's readily adaptable to conventional barbecue cooking. You merely remove the smoke lid from the chimney and replace the stove top with a grill.

The slab for the smoke oven measures 40x60 inches and is made by pouring a 1:2:4 concrete mix into a form made of 2x4's. This 3⅝-inch slab requires between five and six cubic feet of mix. You can save on concrete requirements by throwing in some large rocks, but be sure they don't project above the surface. Use a straight-edged board in leveling off the pour.

Trial Layout

You can begin building the oven itself the next day. First make a trial layout by placing bricks loosely in their approximate position. A grate that will do for your fire chamber can often be found at a junk yard at a fraction of the price new ones cost. It should be approximately 18x20 inches and fit loosely so it can be removed if replacement should at some future date become necessary. You can vary the size of the fire chamber to accommodate the grate you get.

The outside diameter of the 20-inch flue tile section, to be placed in the upper part of the chimney, measures 24 inches. Make a "compass" of two nails with a 12-inch length of connecting string and scribe a circle on the concrete where the chimney is to be centered. Around the circle, place

FOR OVEN'S BASE, make 40x60-inch form of 2x4's, level it, pour concrete, smooth off with form boards.

ON HARDENED BASE, make a "dry run" assembly of bricks, grate to allow for variation in brick size.

GUIDE LINE for chimney is made with string-and-nail in 12-inch radius. Lay bricks outside circle.

LAY BRICKS in ½-inch bed of 1 part mortar cement, 3 parts sand. Cut bricks in half with brickset.

FIRST TWO courses of chimney base are filled in solidly with bricks or rubble, then filled with mortar.

JOINTING TOOL compacts mortar, cuts away excess, smoothens. Use tool when mortar begins to set.

FOURTH COURSE has lining of full bricks set on edge. Removable pan sets in well for drippings.

half bricks in a ½-inch mortar bed. Mortar is made of 1 part mortar cement and 3 parts sand. Mix dry ingredients thoroughly and then add just enough water to give it the consistency of heavy mud. Butter the side of each brick with mortar before placing it alongside its neighbor, and tap it firmly into place.

Fill the inside of the chimney circle solidly with rubble for two courses, then plaster this base over smoothly with mortar.

Side walls of the fire chamber are built up three courses, with a 14-inch wide opening left in front for ashpit access. The grate is placed over the ashpit at the three-course level.

As brickwork progresses, "strike" the joints with a mason's jointing tool, or use a piece of pipe or rounded dowel. In striking, mortar in the joints is compressed and smoothed, the excess falling away.

When you reach the chimney's fourth course, lay a row of whole bricks on edge within the outside circle of half bricks. These edge-set bricks form the lower chimney lining. As on the outside circle, alternate joints of succeeding courses.

The firebox grate is placed about 7½ inches back from the front. Use steel angles to support the bricks that span the ashpit opening. You can buy new 1x1-inch angle stock, or you can pick up the metal rail of an old bed at the junk yard at fractional

FIRE CHAMBER GRATE may be bought new, or at junk yard. A 1x1x24-inch angle spans ashpit.

PLACE FULL BRICKS across ashpit opening, fill ends with bricks cut to size. Cut bricks on board.

TEMPORARILY SUPPORT bricks over opening. Be sure ends of bricks are well-buttered before placing.

SECOND ANGLE behind bricks spanning ashpit opening supports firebrick lining. Check level often.

cost. Use a hacksaw in cutting off two 24-inch lengths to span the opening.

Cut the two outside bricks down to 6 inches for the angle-supported course that spans this opening. This allows two full bricks in the middle, with one end of each firmly supported on the side walls. Place bricks to be cut on a board and rap sharply on the head of a broad-blade chisel with your hammer. Constantly use a spirit level to check the level and plumb of your work, and supplement its use with sighting by eye.

Place a second 1x1x24-inch angle across the ashpit opening behind the first course of bricks. This one supports the firebrick lining course. Two courses of firebrick are placed at the front and two sides of the firebox. They are set on edge. The height of the chimney is now brought up to five courses to match the height of the firebox.

Using your brick trowel, plaster the inside of the chimney with ½ inch of mortar. The mortar covers all irregularities and makes the lining of the chimney smooth and unbroken.

With a third course of firebrick, set flat and overhanging the course below, the top opening of the fire chamber is narrowed down to accommodate a hot plate top. If you cannot salvage a top from an old coal stove at your junk dealer, a ¼-inch steel plate may be substituted, but the stove top arrangement is handier. The one used here

SWITCH FROM firebox to chimney building so that entire structure goes up at once. Grate fits loosely.

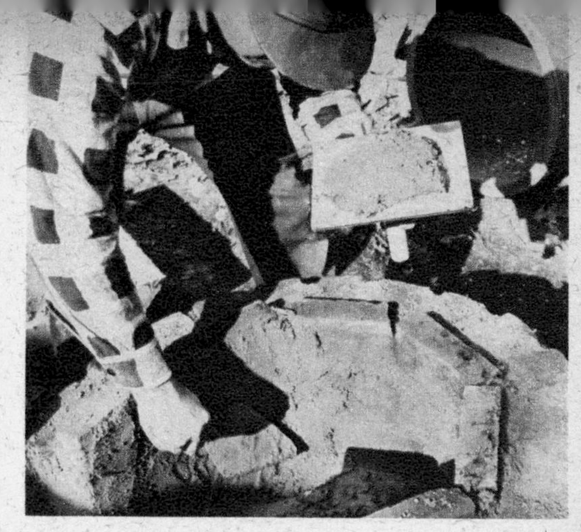

PLASTER INSIDE chimney with ½-inch coat of mortar. This covers irregularities, smoothes lining.

USE EITHER ½-inch rods or angles to support firebrick for firebox top. Lay firebrick with tight joints.

SPACE BETWEEN firebrick and brick facing is filled with mortar. Stove-lid assembly rests on firebricks.

is a two-lid section, but a four-lid section might be used to even better advantage. The stovetop is the place to prepare coffee and warm beans and other vittles to go with your smoke-cooked dinner.

A 26-inch support is needed on either side of the stovetop opening for holding the firebrick where they close in above the firebox. Use either angle stock or a ½-inch reinforcing rod. At stovetop level an 18-inch angle is needed for bridging the opening where chimney meets firebox.

Build the chimney to three courses above the stovetop, and complete plastering of the inside lining with mortar. A two-foot length of 20-inch (24-inch outside diameter) flue tile is now set in place.

Weight of the tile may be near 200 pounds, but you won't find it much of a chore to lift one side of it three or four inches at a time. The trick is to block the tile up on alternate sides with bricks, blocks, or what have you, until you have it at the level desired, then slide it over in position on the chimney. In lieu of this, call on a strong neighbor for help.

Continue the brick work around the tile until the top is reached. The chimney lid for the smoke oven is 24 inches in diameter and is made of ⅛-inch steel, reinforced with a ¾-inch edge band and cross bands on the underside. A four-inch hole cut in the lid is covered by a plate that swivels on a rivet. This is the damper. A handle

USE ANGLE to bridge opening where chimney abuts firebox top. Angle may be any scrap rail.

PLACE BRICKS atop bridge. The 11th course is last before placing flue tile. Complete interior plastering.

GET HELP to lift heavy flue tile in place, or block it up in easy stages until you reach desired height.

METAL LID sells for $12 at local forge. Place mortar cap on brickwork, allow 1/8-inch lid expansion.

on each side of the lid eases its removal. Cost of having such a lid made at your local forge or sheet metal shop will be about $12.

Set the metal lid in position atop the chimney and around it plaster a mortar cap covering the brickwork. Make the cap flush with the top of the lid and level it toward the outside. Jiggle the lid slightly when mortar begins to set so there'll be about 1/8-inch space between lid and mortar for possible expansion.

In use, meat is hung from hooks supported by 1/2-inch rods placed across the flue tile and under the lid. Tidbits, such as shrimp, are smoked in a suspended wire basket. Good eating! •

MATERIALS NEEDED:

- 450 common brick
- 18 firebrick
- 1 20-inch flue tile
- 2 1x1x24-inch angles
- 1 1x1x18-inch angle
- 20 feet 1/2-inch reinforcing rod
- 3 bags mortar cement, 9 cu. ft. sand, 5 1/2 cu. ft. concrete
- stove top, chimney lid, drip pan

BACK-YARD INCINERATOR

This attractive unit contains storage facilities and garbage disposal

By David X. Manners

HANDSOME FACE BRICK makes a structure that dresses up your back yard, as the photo shows.

CHIMNEY CAP prevents rain from wetting refuse in unit. Make cap as described in text.

YOU can solve the twin problems of where to burn trash, and where to store lawnmower, garden furniture or tools, with a single unit. By using an attractive face brick in the structure's construction you can further enhance its pleasing design.

A six-inch concrete slab affords firm support for the project and provides the floor for both the storage section and the ashpit. The slab is reinforced with six-inch mesh placed at the halfway point.

The partition wall between storage and incinerator sections is of masonry block. The incinerator may be lined with either hard-burned or firebrick. For the incinerator grate, use either a 12x24-inch cast iron affair, supported on a ½x2-inch steel strip set between fourth and fifth brick courses, or—less expensively—mortar ⅝-inch rods, on three-inch centers, between those courses.

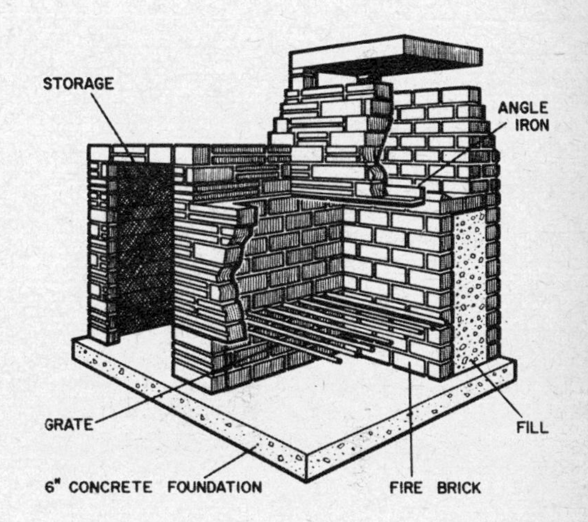

Chimney Support

Support brickwork over the ashpit opening with a steel T. A 2x2-inch angle supports the chimney masonry at the point where smoke enters the flue. Note the piece of angled brick at the chimney throat and the smoke shelf behind it. These serve as a baffle against downdrafts and insure

STORAGE UNIT DOOR is made of heavy aluminum with edges bent over ½ inch for reinforcement.

DOOR OPENING is framed with 2x4's nailed to mortar joints. Hasp closure permits padlocking.

SPACE IS ideally suited for storing power mower, gas can, etc. Grade-level slab makes easy entry.

proper operation of the incinerator unit.

The lid covering the incinerator opening, a ⅛x16x16-inch steel plate, can be fabricated at any local forge or metal working shop for about $5. The four-inch lengths of steel rod welded to corners of the plate serve as hinge pins. The pins are set into eye-bolts cemented between bricks. Another length of rod welded to the front of the plate at midway point serves as lid handle.

The interior of the chimney base is filled with rubble or compacted dirt. Finish the inside of the chimney smooth with a coating of mortar. A spark arrestor screen safeguards against fire hazards, and a chimney cap prevents wetting down of unburned trash by rain.

A ¾x24-inch pipe set as a threshold in the storage section protects the edge of the slab against damage and also serves as a stop for the door. Door is of aluminum

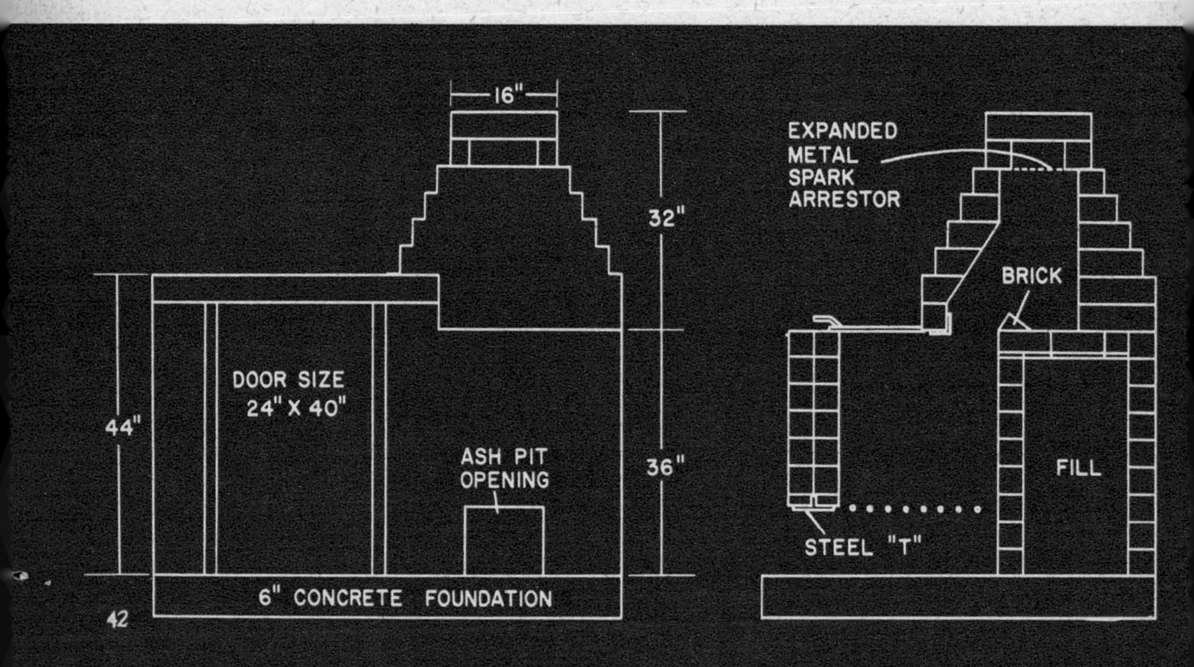

INCINERATOR LID is ⅛x16x16-inch steel. Rod pins set in eyebolts act as hinges. Cost: $5 at local forge.

INSTALL LID with sufficient clearance so it can be tilted back slightly when open, as shown above.

and can be made at any sheet metal shop. However, you can make an equally satisfactory door of tongue-and-groove boards, joined on the inside face by battens. Door opening is framed on each side by 2x4's nailed to mortar joints. The front edges of the 2x4's are rabbeted so that when the door is closed it fits flush.

The opening above the door is bridged by a 2x2x36-inch steel angle. Roof over the storage section is a 4-inch concrete slab poured after brick facing is in place and has set hard. The facing serves as outside edges of the slab form. The bottom of the form is made of tongue-and-groove boards set across the span and left in place after the slab is poured. These boards are supported underneath with props at 16-inch intervals until the slab has set. The slab is reinforced with ½-inch rods, laid checkerboard style, with intersections, wired together. Space rods a foot apart. •

MATERIALS NEEDED:

- 700 standard-size bricks (8¼x3⅝x2¼ inch approximately)
- 15 masonry blocks
- 3 sacks portland cement
- 3 sacks lime
- ½ yard sand
- 15 cu. ft. concrete for foundation
- 8 cu. ft. concrete for storage roof and chimney cap

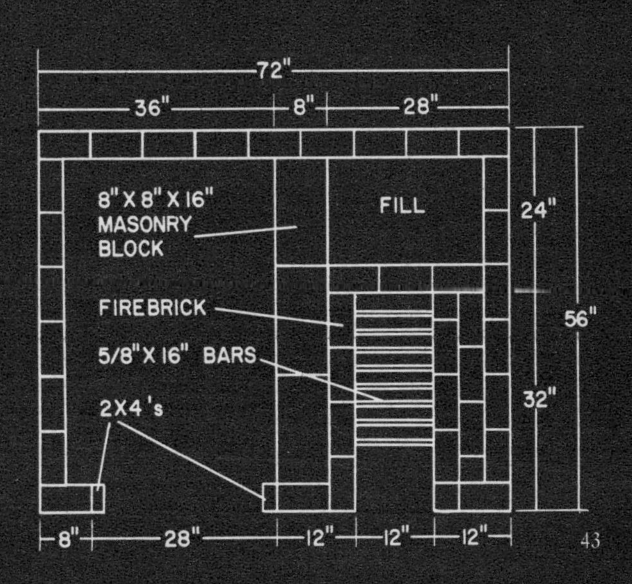

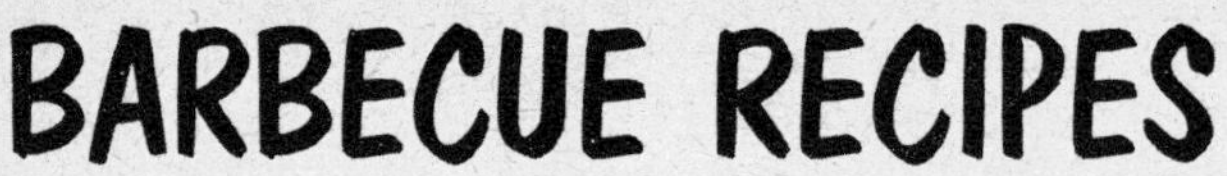

BARBECUE RECIPES

These are tempting, tasty and easy-to-make

By Hyla O'Connor

Triple Burgers

1½ pounds ground beef
Salt and pepper
2 tablespoons butter
1 onion, chopped
½ green pepper, chopped
Sliced enriched bread

Season beef with salt and pepper. Pat out between 2 pieces of waxed paper into an 8-inch square. Cut the square into fourths. Broil on a grill over hot coals until brown on both sides. Melt butter in a skillet. Add onion and pepper and cook gently until tender. Season with salt and pepper. Place browned beef square on a slice of bread. Top with a second slice of bread. Spoon on some of the onion mixture and top with a third slice of bread. Makes 4 triple burgers.

Deviled Spareribs

6 pounds spareribs
2 tablespoons salad oil
2 tablespoons tarragon vinegar
½ cup fine enriched bread crumbs

Cut spareribs into serving size pieces. Brush with salad oil combined with vinegar. Dip in fine bread crumbs. Grill over hot coals, turning frequently until brown and crisp on both sides. Serve with Devil Sauce. Makes 6 servings.

Devil Sauce

3 tablespoons minced green onions
3 tablespoons butter or margarine
¼ cup lemon juice
2 teaspoons Worcestershire sauce
2 teaspoons prepared mustard
Dash of Tabasco
1 10¾-ounce can beef gravy

Sauté onions in butter until soft. Blend in lemon juice, Worcestershire sauce, mustard, Tabasco and beef gravy. Heat through. Serve hot with spareribs.

Outdoor Barbecue Sauce

½ cup beer
2 tablespoons vinegar
2 tablespoons Worcestershire sauce
2 tablespoons lemon juice
1 cup chili sauce

Roto-Broil

Combine all ingredients in a large beer mug. Mix well. Brush hamburgers with a long-handled brush while cooking.

Luncheon Meat Kebab

2 cans (12 ounces each) luncheon meat
Medium onions
Green peppers
2 cans (4 ounces each) button mushrooms

Cut luncheon meat in half and then in thirds to make 18 cubes. Cut onions into wedges and green peppers into 1-inch squares. Drain mushrooms; alternate ingredients as desired on large skewers. Place on grill and cook over medium heat. Turn occasionally, brush with barbecue sauce and cook until meat is desired brownness. Makes about 8 to 10 Kebabs.

Barbecue Sauce

2 medium onions, chopped
1 green pepper, chopped
⅔ cup sweet pickle relish
⅔ cup vinegar
2 cups chili sauce
¼ cup firmly packed brown sugar
1 tablespoon prepared mustard
½ teaspoon Tabasco sauce

Combine all ingredients for barbecue sauce in saucepan. Bring to boiling point and simmer 20 minutes. Use to brush Kabobs. Makes 3 cups sauce.

Barbecue Beans

3 medium onions, sliced
2 green peppers, chopped
⅔ cup sweet pickle relish
½ cup vinegar
2 cups chili sauce
¼ cup brown sugar
1 tablespoon mustard
½ teaspoon Tabasco sauce
3 1-pound cans baked beans

Combine all ingredients except beans in a saucepan and simmer 10 minutes. Heat beans in a heavy skillet; stir in barbecue sauce. Heat and serve. Makes 12 servings.

Hamburgers—to suit everyone

1. Fry 1 pound hamburger and 1 large chopped onion in a heavy skillet until light brown. Add 1 8-ounce can tomato sauce, $\frac{3}{4}$ cup water, 1 teaspoon salt, $\frac{1}{8}$ teaspoon pepper and $\frac{1}{4}$ teaspoon garlic salt. Cook, uncovered for 20 minutes, stirring often. Split hard rolls and fill centers with meat mixture. Serves 8.

2. Cut 2 large green peppers and 1 large red pepper into chunks. Fry in a little salad oil in a heavy skillet until tender. Shape 1 pound hamburger into a steak $1\frac{1}{2}$ inches thick and 3 inches wide. Broil on a rack over red-hot coals to desired doneness. Cut into 8 slices. Cut a loaf of French bread into 4-inch pieces. Split and butter each piece. Top with 2 slices of steak and $\frac{1}{4}$ of the green peppers. Season to taste. Makes 4 sandwiches.

3. For each serving, shape around the end of a green stick $\frac{1}{4}$ pound hamburger seasoned with minced onion, salt and pepper. Wrap diagonally with a slice of bacon; pin with toothpicks. Cook slowly over a bed of hot coals, turning often, until bacon is crisp. Remove picks and slip meat from stick into a split, toasted frankfurter roll.

4. Mix together $1\frac{1}{2}$ pounds ground beef, $1\frac{1}{2}$ teaspoons salt, $\frac{1}{4}$ teaspoon black pepper, $\frac{1}{2}$ teaspoon monosodium glutamate and 1 teaspoon Worcestershire sauce. Shape into 8 thin patties. Place a thin slice of sharp cheese on each of 4 patties. Cover with remaining 4 patties and pinch edges together to seal. Grill over hot coals until desired doneness, turning just once. Allow about 5 minutes for medium rare burgers. Serve between toasted hamburger buns.

5. Combine 1 pound ground beef, $\frac{1}{4}$ cup sour cream, $\frac{1}{4}$ cup chili sauce, 1 teaspoon Worcestershire sauce and 1 teaspoon monosodium glutamate. Shape into 4 patties. Cook on a grill over hot coals to desired doneness. Serve on toasted hamburger rolls.

6. Lightly mix 1 pound ground chuck, 1 teaspoon salt, $\frac{1}{4}$ teaspoon pepper, $\frac{1}{2}$ cup minced fresh mushrooms, and $\frac{1}{2}$ cup grated Cheddar cheese. Shape into 4 to 6 patties, grill over hot coals to desired doneness. Serve between toasted hamburger buns.

7. Lightly toss 1 pound ground beef, 2 tablespoons catchup, 1 teaspoon salt, 1 teaspoon horse-radish, 1 tablespoon minced onion, 1 teaspoon Worcestershire sauce and 1 teaspoon prepared mustard. Shape into 4 or 6 patties. Wrap a bacon slice around each patty and fasten with a toothpick. Grill over hot coals. Serve between toasted hamburger buns.

Over the Coals Steak

Have a large enough fire to start with to have a good bed of coals, but don't start cooking until the flames die down and there is left only a bed of glowing coals. The grill should be 3 to 5 inches from the coals, depending on the thickness of the steaks and the degree of doneness; the thicker the steaks or the more well done you want them, the farther they should be from the coals.

Choose top quality steaks at least 1-inch thick. Tender steaks such as porterhouse, T-bone, sirloin or club are the best choices for broiling. Trim off excess fat, leaving only a thin edge of fat. Score the fat to prevent curling during cooking. Broil one side until well browned. Turn with tongs, never a fork because piercing the meat releases the juices, and season. Broil second side to the desired degree of doneness. Season and serve.

It is not possible to give an exact time for broiling steaks, variations in heat and thickness of steak must be taken into consideration. Roughly, for a 1-inch steak it takes about 20 minutes for medium rare and about 40 minutes to cook a 2-inch steak medium rare. Test for doneness by cutting near bone and noting color of meat.

Barbecued Chicken on a Spit

- 2 tablespoons butter or margarine
- 1 medium onion, chopped
- 1 clove garlic, chopped
- ½ cup chopped celery
- ¼ cup chopped green pepper
- 1 No. 2 can tomatoes
- 1 can (6-ounce) tomato paste
- 1 bay leaf
- 3 tablespoons brown sugar
- 2 teaspoons dry mustard
- ⅓ cup vinegar
- ½ teaspoon cloves
- ½ teaspoon allspice
- 2 slices lemon
- 1½ teaspoons salt
- 2 teaspoons Tabasco
- 4-pound roasting chicken

Melt butter, add onion and garlic and cook until onion is tender but not brown. Add remaining ingredients, except chicken, and simmer 30 minutes. Let stand until cooled. Wipe chicken with a damp cloth. Pour sauce over chicken and let stand about 30 minutes. Remove chicken from sauce and place on spit of barbecue. Cook, turning every ten minutes or so. Baste frequently with sauce. Cook from 1 to 1½ hours, or until leg of chicken is tender and not pink. Makes 4 servings.

Broiled Chicken Deluxe

Split 2½ pound broilers in half. Break at joints so that chicken lies flat. Rub entire surface of chicken with a cut lemon, squeezing out some juice occasionally. Sprinkle with salt, pepper and paprika. Sprinkle with about 2 tablespoons of sugar. Lay chicken on a greased grid, cut side down over hot coals. Baste occasionally with melted butter and turn pieces frequently to insure even browning. The chicken will be done in about 35 minutes and when no pink shows at the bone.

Campfire Chicken

Cut a frying chicken into serving pieces. Wipe with a damp cloth and brush each piece with melted bacon fat. Sprinkle with salt, pepper, chopped chives and chopped parsley. Lay one or two pieces of chicken out on large squares of heavy duty aluminum foil. Add a few slices of mushrooms, a thin slice of onion and a drained canned

or whole peeled fresh tomato to each packet. Bring foil up over food and double fold all edges to form a tight packet. Place packets on grate over hot coals and cook 35 to 40 minutes. Turn packets after about 15 minutes and cook the same time on second side. Turn again and cook 10 minutes or so longer on first side. Remove from fire and serve one packet to each person.

Spicy Chicken

- 2 2 to 2½ pound broiling chickens, split
- 1 cup salad oil
- ¼ cup vinegar
- 1 tablespoon horse-radish
- ¼ cup chili sauce
- ½ teaspoon dry mustard
- 1 teaspoon salt
- 1 clove garlic, crushed

Remove necks and backbones of chickens with a poultry shears or sharp knife. Wash and dry thoroughly; arrange in a large flat dish. Combine remaining ingredients and pour over chicken. Let stand in refrigerator at least 2 hours, turning chicken pieces several times. Drain halves and place on grill over hot coals. Broil quickly on both sides to seal in juices. Move away from very hot coals and continue to broil, turning and basting frequently with sauce until well browned and flesh is tender when pierced with a fork. About 40 minutes in all. Makes 4 servings.

Chicken with Tomato

- 1 4 to 5 pound fowl, cut in pieces
- ⅓ cup flour
- 4 tablespoons shortening
- ¼ pound sliced mushrooms
- 1 No. 303 can tomatoes
- 2 cups tomato juice
- 2 teaspoons salt
- ¼ teaspoon pepper
- ½ teaspoon thyme
- 1 teaspoon sugar
- 12 small white onions
- 1 package frozen lima beans
- 6 green pepper rings

Place chicken pieces and flour in a paper bag and shake until chicken is thoroughly coated with flour. Heat fat in a heavy Dutch oven; add chicken and brown well on all sides. Add mushrooms, tomatoes, tomato juice, salt, pepper, thyme and sugar. Cover and cook slowly about 1 hour. Add onions and continue cooking about 15 minutes. Add lima beans and green pepper and cook about 15 minutes longer. Makes 6 servings.

Near East Chicken

- 2 3-pound chickens, cut in pieces
- ¼ cup salad oil
- ½ pound brown rice
- ½ pound almonds, blanched and chopped
- 2 large onions
- 2 seedless oranges
- 3 cups milk
- 3 tablespoons chopped pimiento
- ⅛ teaspoon pepper
- ¼ teaspoon dried thyme
- 2 teaspoons salt
- Pinch of sugar
- Dash cayenne pepper

Wipe chicken pieces with a damp cloth. Roll each piece in flour. Heat salad oil in a very large heavy skillet. Brown chicken pieces quickly on all sides. Remove from pan. Add rice and almonds to drippings in the pan. Cook, stirring constantly, until rice is golden brown. Put onions and oranges through coarse blade of food chopper. Add to rice in pan. Smooth mixture out in pan. Arrange chicken on top of rice mixture. Add remaining ingredients. Cover tightly and cook on outdoor grill about 1 hour, or until chicken is tender. Makes 8 servings.

South African Rock Lobster Association

South African Rock Lobster Kebabs

4 (5 to 7 ounces) South African rock lobster tails
1 small can pineapple chunks
1 small can mushroom crowns
1 green pepper, cut in 1-inch squares
2 firm tomatoes, quartered
8 small white onions
½ cup butter, melted
1 teaspoon Angostura bitters

Thaw South African rock lobster tails. With scissors, cut undershell around edges and remove. Pull out meat and cut each tail in 4 pieces. Alternate ingredients on skewers to suit your fancy, using 4 chunks of lobster for each skewer. Combine butter and bitters and brush each kebab liberally. Broil over hot coals 5 to 6 minutes, or until lobster meat loses its transparency and is tender. Turn skewers over, brush again with butter mixture and broil about 1 minute more. Serve with remaining butter. Makes 4 servings.

Herb Barbecued Rock Lobster Tails

4 to 6 South African rock lobster tails
½ cup butter, melted
1 envelope herb or garlic salad dressing mix
1 lemon, sliced

Thaw rock lobster tails. With scissors, cut undershell around edges and remove. Grasp tail in both hands and bend backwards toward shell side to crack in 3 places. Or insert a small skewer in meat to keep the tail flat. Arrange on grill, shell side down, some distance from hot coals. Cook about 5 minutes. Combine melted butter and salad dressing mix. Brush flesh side of tails liberally with this mixture. Turn flesh side toward the heat and continue broiling about 5 minutes, or until meat loses its transparency and is tender. Serve with remaining butter mix. Garnish with lemon slices. Makes 4 to 6 servings.

Barbecued Grilled Fish

4 fish steaks, cut ¾-inch thick
2 tablespoons lemon juice
½ cup salad oil
1 teaspoon savory salt

Place fish steaks in a shallow pan. Combine lemon juice, oil and savory salt; pour over fish. Let stand in the refrigerator 2 hours. Arrange fish in a folding wire broiler. Brush well with marinade. Grill close to hot coals 3 minutes, or until fish is golden. Brush with marinade, turn and grill until fish is tender and golden browned. Makes 4 servings.

Broiled Stuffed Fish

1 3- to 4-pound bass
1½ cups bread cubes
½ teaspoon salt
⅛ teaspoon pepper
¼ teaspoon thyme
½ onion, minced
½ cup butter or margarine, melted
2 tablespoons lemon juice
1 No. 2 can white onions
1 can (3-ounce) mushrooms
Salt and pepper
Chopped parsley

Have fish cleaned with head and tail removed. Rub inside with salt. Combine bread cubes, salt, pepper, thyme, onion and ¼ cup of the butter. Place mixture in body cavity of fish. Bind fish in about 3 places with string. Tear off a large piece of heavy duty foil and fold double to make a double thick wrap for the fish. Place fish on foil. Pour over it the remaining melted butter and lemon juice. Add onions and mushrooms. Sprinkle with salt, pepper and parsley. Bring the foil up and over the fish and seal edges together tightly with a double fold. Place package of fish on grate over medium hot coals. Grill rather slowly, allowing 15 to 20 minutes for each pound of fish. Turn two or three times during cooking period. When cooked, place package on a large serving tray, open foil and serve. Makes 6 to 8 servings.

Steamed Clams

Allow 15 to 25 clams for each person. Scrub clams thoroughly in plenty of clean water. Place clams in a large kettle with about ½ inch of water. Cover tightly and steam 6 to 10 minutes or until clams are just open. Do not overcook. Serve clams on plates with melted butter or margarine, seasoned with a few drops of lemon juice. Clam broth should be strained and served piping hot with the clams.

Barbecued Shrimp

½ cup minced onion
¼ cup butter or margarine
1 cup ketchup
1 cup chili sauce
2 tablespoons wine vinegar
1 teaspoon Worcestershire sauce
1 teaspoon prepared horseradish
Dash of salt
3 cups shelled shrimp

Cook onion in butter in a heavy skillet until golden brown. Add remaining ingredients except shrimp. Bring to a boil and cook 20 minutes. Add shrimp and simmer 5 minutes. Makes 4 servings.

Broiled Lobster

To kill the lobster, insert a sharp knife between the body and tail shells; this severs the spinal cord. Place lobster on back and make a deep cut lengthwise from head to end of tail. Open and remove stomach, dark vein and liver. Crack large claws. Brush meat with melted butter or margarine and place cut side down on rack over hot coals. Cook about 5 minutes. Turn cut side up. Brush with melted butter and season with salt and pepper. Broil 10 to 15 minutes or until meat is tender. Time, of course, depends on size of lobster and distance from heat. Serve with melted butter with a squeeze of lemon juice added to it.

Broiled Oysters

26 shell oysters
½ teaspoon salt
⅛ teaspoon pepper
½ cup bread crumbs
2 tablespoons butter or margarine

Shuck and drain oysters; place in deep half of shells. Sprinkle with salt, pepper and buttered bread crumbs. Place on grill and cook over very hot coals until edges of oysters curl. Makes 6 servings.

Skewered Shrimp

- 2 pounds jumbo shrimp
- 2 cloves garlic, minced
- 1 chopped onion
- ¼ cup lemon juice
- 1 teaspoon dried basil
- 1 teaspoon dried mustard
- 1 teaspoon salt
- ½ cup salad oil

Without removing the shells, cut the back of each shrimp with kitchen scissors. Wash under running water to remove black vein. Place in a bowl. Combine remaining ingredients and pour over shrimp. Let stand in refrigerator several hours, turning shrimp occasionally. Thread shrimp on thin metal skewers, allowing 5 shrimp for each skewer. Grill about 5 minutes over hot coals, basting with marinade and turning once. Makes 6 servings.

Far Island Steak

- 5-pound sirloin steak, cut 1½-inches thick
- ½ cup soy sauce
- 2 tablespoons sugar
- 2 cloves garlic, crushed
- ½ teaspoon ginger
- ¼ cup finely chopped onion
- ¼ cup water

Score the fat around edge of steak to prevent curling. Prick meat on both sides with a fork. Place in a large flat dish. Combine remaining ingredients and pour over meat. Let stand in refrigerator at least 1 hour; turn meat several times. Drain meat thoroughly and place on grill. Broil 10 to 12 minutes on each side for rare, 12 to 14 minutes for medium rare, 14 to 16 minutes for well done. Remove steak to a cutting board and cut in thin diagonal slices. Makes 4 to 6 servings.

Barbecued Ham Slice

- 1 1-inch thick slice ready-to-eat ham
- ½ cup ketchup
- 2 tablespoons vinegar
- 2 tablespoons brown sugar
- 1 tablespoon Worcestershire sauce

Score fat on edge of ham to prevent curling. Combine remaining ingredients. Brush ham with sauce. Place on a grill over hot coals; broil 15 to 20 minutes, turning and brushing frequently with the sauce. Makes 4 servings.

Stuffed Flank Steak

- 1 flank steak (1½ to 2 pounds)
- 1 cup soft bread crumbs
- ¼ cup chopped onion
- ½ teaspoon sage
- ½ cup chopped celery
- ½ cup shredded carrots
- Salt and pepper
- 2 tablespoons beef broth
- ¼ cup flour
- ¼ cup salad oil
- 1 cup water

Make shallow criss-cross cuts with a sharp knife in fibers of the steak. Combine bread crumbs, onions, sage, celery, carrots, ¼ teaspoon salt, dash of pepper and beef broth. Sprinkle salt and pepper on one side of the steak. Spread bread mixture over steak. Roll up tightly crosswise. Fasten with skewers or tie with string. Roll in seasoned flour. Brown in hot salad oil in a heavy skillet. Add water. Cover skillet tightly and simmer over moderate heat about 1½ hours. Makes 4 to 6 servings.

Barbecued Pork Chops

- 6 thick loin or rib pork chops
- 1 large onion, chopped
- 1 large green pepper, chopped
- 2 tablespoons brown sugar
- 2 tablespoons lemon juice
- 1 tablespoon Worcestershire sauce
- 1 teaspoon chili powder
- ½ teaspoon salt

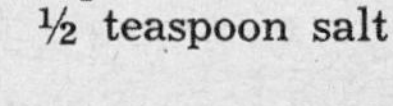

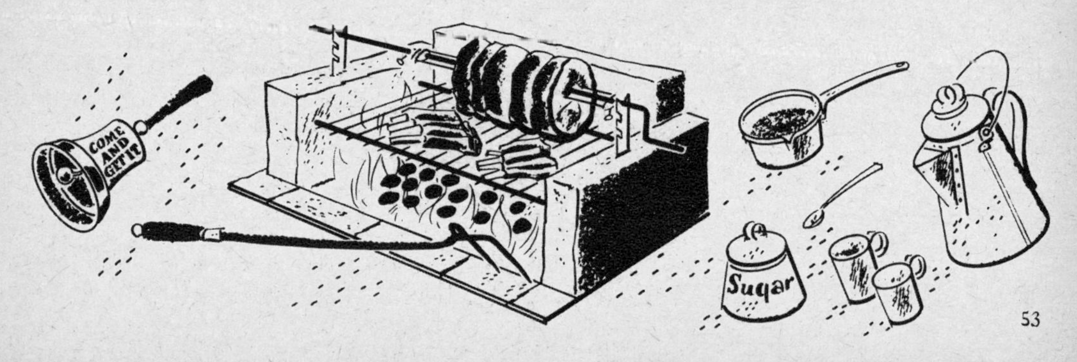

½ teaspoon mustard
1 cup water
1 can (8 ounces) tomato sauce

Trim all but a thin layer of fat from the chops. Heat a large skillet; brown chops well on both sides; remove from pan. Sauté onion and green pepper in drippings in pan about 10 minutes, or until tender. Drain off any fat. Add brown sugar, lemon juice, Worcestershire sauce, chili powder, salt, mustard and water. Mix well. Arrange chops in skillet; pour tomato sauce around chops. Cover pan tightly and simmer 45 to 60 minutes or until chops are tender. Makes 6 servings.

Lamb and Vegetables

2 pounds boneless lamb shoulder
¼ cup flour
2 tablespoons shortening
1½ teaspoons salt
Dash of pepper
3 cups water
1 teaspoon fresh dill
2 cloves garlic, crushed
½ teaspoon Kitchen Bouquet
½ pound green beans, cut in half crosswise
8 small carrots, cleaned
1 small head cauliflower, separated in pieces

Cut meat in 1½-inch cubes. Roll in flour to coat evenly. Heat shortening in a Dutch oven; add meat and brown well on all sides. Add salt, pepper, water, dill and garlic. Cook slowly for 2 hours or until meat is almost tender. Add Kitchen Bouquet, green beans and carrots and cook about 15 minutes. Add cauliflower and cook 15 minutes longer. Makes 8 servings.

Broiled Flank Steak

Remove excess fat and skin from a 1½- to 2-pound flank steak. Place steak on a heated grill over very hot coals. Broil 8 minutes on first side, turn and broil 5 more minutes. Season to taste. Slice in very thin slices, crosswise at a 45 degree angle.

This steak looks tough, but is very ten-

Tabasco

der if you remember to cut it at an angle, through the muscle fibers. Makes 4 to 6 servings.

Shortribs

- 3½ to 4 pounds beef shortribs
- ¾ cup water
- 2 tablespoons vinegar
- ½ teaspoon dry mustard
- 1 teaspoon chili powder
- 1 teaspoon salt
- 1 teaspoon pepper
- 1 small onion, minced
- 1 clove garlic, minced
- 2 teaspoons sugar
- ¼ teaspoon Tabasco

Have shortribs cut in 2-inch pieces. Place ribs in a shallow pan. Combine remaining ingredients in a saucepan. Bring to a boil and simmer 5 minutes. Cool. Pour over ribs and let stand in the refrigerator at least 2 hours. Place ribs on rack over glowing coals. Cook about 25 minutes for medium rare, basting frequently with sauce and turning to brown on all sides. Makes 4 servings.

Spareribs

- 3 to 4 pounds spareribs
- 1 chicken bouillon cube
- 1 cup boiling water
- 1 teaspoon salt
- 2 cloves garlic, minced
- ⅓ cup ketchup
- ⅓ cup soy sauce
- ⅓ cup honey

Have ribs cracked down the middle and cut into 3-rib sections to enable easy turning. Dissolve bouillon cube in boiling water. Add remaining ingredients and pour over ribs in a shallow pan. Let stand in refrigerator about 2 hours, turning occasionally. Place ribs on grill over hot coals. Cook, basting with sauce and turning frequently, about 25 minutes, or until ribs are well done. Makes about 4 servings.

Steak Sandwiches

Select a 2-inch thick chuck steak. Trim off excess fat and slash outer edge of fat to prevent curling. Sprinkle all surfaces with

meat tenderizer, according to directions on the package. Cook 3 to 5 inches from glowing coals, turning just once during cooking. Test for doneness by cutting near bone and noting color. Cut long loaves of French bread lengthwise into halves. Spread cut surfaces with butter or brush with melted garlic butter. Cut grilled steak across the grain into thin slices and place on bottom halves of bread loaves. Cover with bread tops. Cut crosswise on a slant into individual portions about 3 inches thick.

Shish Kebab

- 5- to 7-pound leg of lamb
- 1/3 cup salad oil
- 1/3 cup vinegar
- 1/2 teaspoon pepper
- 1 teaspoon oregano
- 1/2 teaspoon thyme
- 1 teaspoon salt
- 6 green peppers, cut in 2-inch pieces
- 16 to 20 small onions, peeled and halved

Have bone removed from leg of lamb. Cut lamb into 2-inch chunks. Combine salad oil, vinegar, pepper, oregano, thyme and salt. Pour over lamb chunks in a shallow pan. Let stand in refrigerator several hours or over night. Alternate lamb chunks, green pepper pieces and onions on 8 to 10 very long metal skewers. Brush with marinade. Grill over hot coals 10 to 15 minutes, turning often, until lamb is brown and tender. Makes 8 to 10 servings. •

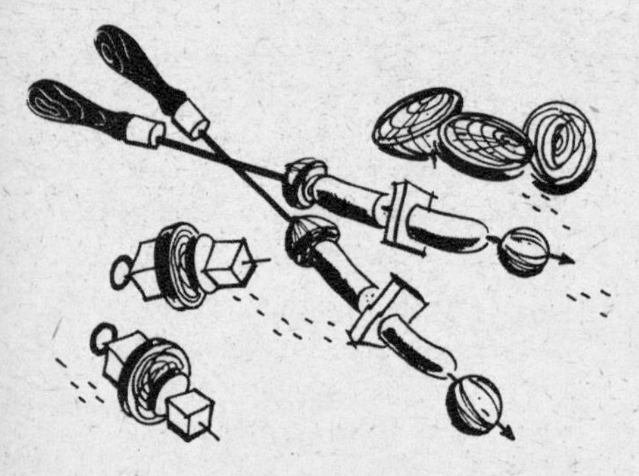

National Meat Canners Association

PICNIC SET

This table-and-bench combination is very easy to build

By David X. Manners

GOOD DESIGN and usefulness of this picnic set has made it an excellent furnishing for outdoor parties.

A GOOD and spacious table is essential in outdoor dining. Equally important is convenient seating. A rugged weatherproof table and matching benches is the perfect answer to these requirements. Construction is so simple it can readily be done with hand tools alone, though—naturally—power tools make it easier.

To withstand the rigors of rain and sun, the dining set should be made of redwood or cedar. Nails should be galvanized and screws, bolts and nuts should be cadmium plated. You can use 5/4-inch stock, but it's inclined to have a skimpy look, particularly if your table is over five feet long. Hefty two-inch stock costs only a little more and is worth the difference. Screw-and-bolt assembly makes it easy to take the set apart for out-of-season storage, if desired.

Construction of the table and benches is almost identical. The only real difference is in the size of the parts. Make the table first, to familiarize yourself with the operation. You can then make the two benches together on a production basis, cutting and drilling all pieces in a single run.

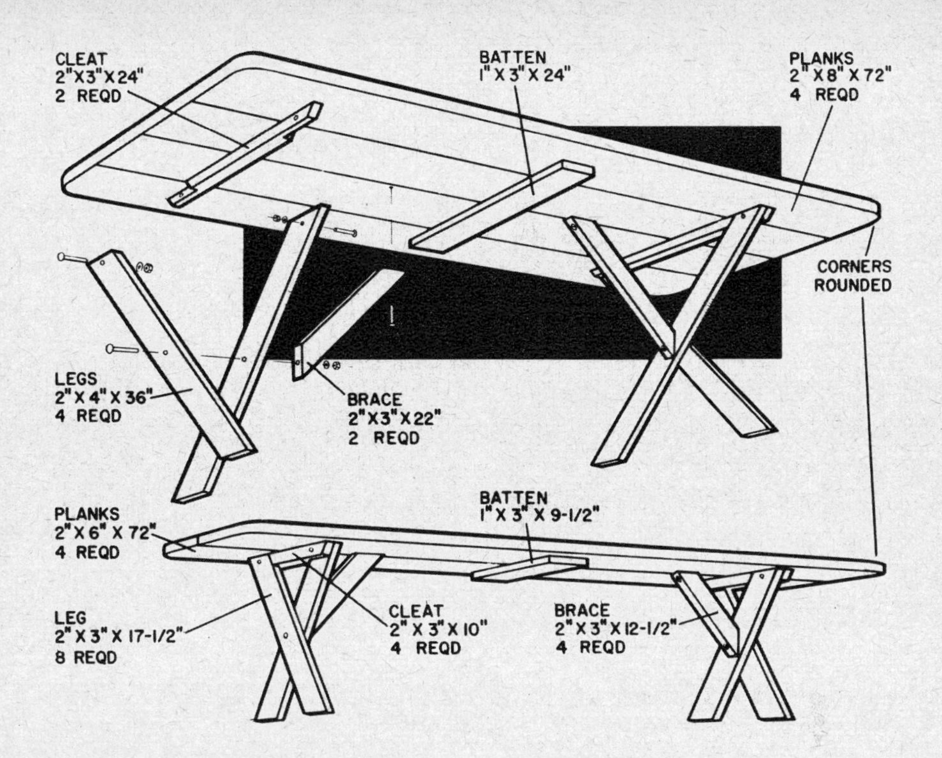

Table legs are cut from 2x4's. Cut four pieces 36 inches long. Measure back three inches from the end along the *top* edge and three inches from the other end along the *bottom* edge. Draw a diagonal line from each point back across the board to the near corner. Cut off the triangular pieces thus marked. Draw a line along the length of the board at its middle. On the line drill one ¼-inch hole 1⅛ inches in from the edge and drill another hole 8¾ inches in.

Two leg braces, each 21¾ inches long, are cut from 2x3 stock. The diagonal cut at each end of these leg braces is exactly a 45-degree miter, and can be cut on your table or radial saw with settings at this point. Note that, unlike the leg pieces where the slanting end cuts parallel each other, these end cuts toe inward.

On each of the braces mark a point 2½

MEASURE 3 inches from each leg end, make slant cuts. Cuts at opposite ends of legs are parallel.

END CUTS for leg braces are 45-degree miters. Note that slant cuts at opposite ends are not parallel.

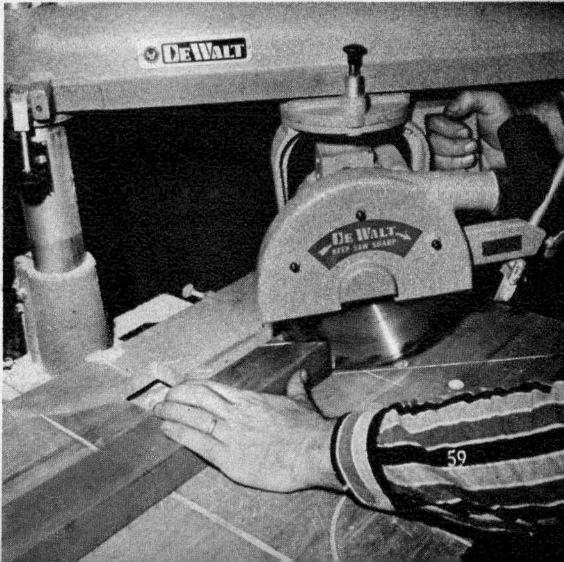

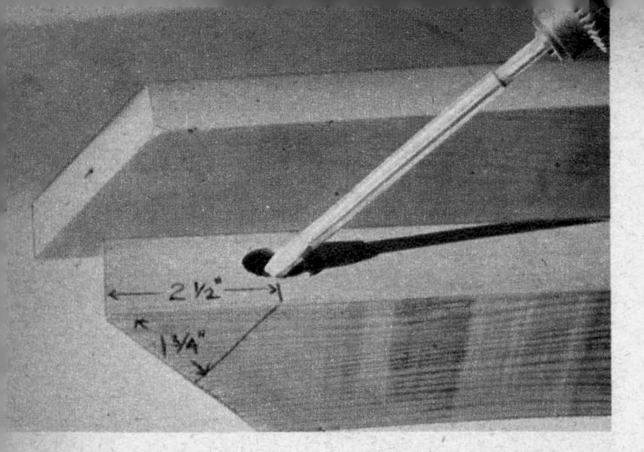

DRILL ¼-inch hole through each brace end, then enlarge hole with ½-inch bit to depth of ½ inch.

CLEATS for table and benches are made by cutting blocks out of alternate sides of a chamfered 2x3.

inches in from the end along the long edge. Drill a ¼-inch hole through the middle of the board at this point to the midpoint of the slanting edge. Since this slant edge measures 3½ inches, midpoint is at the 1¾-inch mark. Enlarge the two holes on the top edges to a depth of ½ inch, using a ½-inch drill.

Each pair of table legs is fastened to the tabletop by means of a cleat. Cleats are cut from a length of 2x3 measuring 23¾ inches. Each end of the cleat is chamfered (a bevel that does not go the full thickness of the board), and the board is ripped down the middle to a point 5⅝ inches from either end. Cross cut from opposite edges to the middle of the board, then remove 5⅝-inch blocks. Drill holes through the edge of the cleat two inches in from each end, at midpoint, using a ¼-inch bit.

Planks for the table top are 2x8's six feet long, with ¼-inch spaces between. Use a compass set to a 1¾-inch radius and mark the outside corners of the two planks forming the tabletop sides for rounding off. Four planks are needed to make a table approximately 30 inches wide. Round over all plank edges, particularly outside edges.

Solidly nail a 1x3 batten 24 inches long at the midpoint of the table. Nail cleats to the underside of the tabletop at a point six inches in from each end, and approximately three inches from each side.

Insert a ¼x6-inch machine screw or carriage bolt through the midpoint holes

BOTH table and bench cleats are attached six inches from end. Planks are spaced ¼ inch apart.

MATERIALS NEEDED:

1 4 ft. 1x3
2 12 ft. 2x3
1 12 ft. 2x4
2 12 ft. 2x6
2 12 ft. 2x8

Two ¼x6-inch machine screws or carriage bolts—cadmium plated

Four ¼x3½-inch machine screws—cadmium plated

Two 2-inch flathead wood screws—cadmium plated

in a pair of crossed legs and on through the hole cut in the slant end of a brace. If you are using carriage bolts, you'll need ten or more washers at the end of the bolt before turning on the nut or you'll find it impossible to tighten the nut. Use a flathead wood screw two inches long for attaching the other end of the brace to the table. Attach legs to cleats with ¼x3½-inch machine screws.

With table construction and assembly complete, proceed with making the two benches. Out of 2x3, for braces cut four pieces 12½ inches long, for legs eight pieces 17½ inches long, and for cleats four pieces 10 inches long. Out of 1x3, cut two battens 9½ inches long. Provide four 6-foot 2x6's for the bench seats.

Leg Assembly

To complete the legs, mark off one inch from the ends, on alternate sides. From the marks, draw a line across to the near corner and trim off the triangular piece thus outlined. Finished leg measures 16⅜ inches long. Mark a center line down the board and drill two ¼-inch holes, one ⅞ inch and the other 8¾ inches from one end. Cut all eight legs to these dimensions.

To complete the braces, measure off 1½ inches from either end along one edge, draw lines across the board to the near corner and trim off the triangles thus marked. Brace will now measure 12½ inches along the top side and 9½ inches along the bottom. The cut is a 45-degree miter, and can be made by simple setting on table or radial saw. Drill ¼-inch holes through the top side of each brace 2½ inches from either end and angled so the holes come out at midpoint on the slant ends. Position one of these holes ½ inch from the front face and the other ½ inch from the back face. This is necessary to prevent holes from falling over the crack between the two bench planks when attachment is made. Enlarge the holes with a ½-inch drill to a depth of ½ inch. Cut all four braces to these specifications.

To complete the cleats, first chamfer (partially bevel) the ends. Draw a center line down the board and rip four inches along it from either end. Now cut in from alternate sides of the board to remove four-inch blocks. Centered along the side of the board, drill ½-inch holes 1⅞ inches from either end.

Round off outside corners of planks to a 1¾-inch radius, and join each pair of planks with a cross batten nailed to the plank's underside at midpoint. Allow a space of ¼ inch between planks.

Nail cleats six inches in from either end. Join legs with a ¼x6-inch bolt and attach brace before threading on nut. Join legs to cleat with ¼x3½-inch bolts and attach brace to planks with a 2-inch wood screw.

Give picnic set a finish sanding and a coat of redwood sealer. Approximate cost: $20 to $30 depending upon locality and lumber. •

DRAWINGS BELOW give dimensions of parts. Note: table and bench braces are attached with ¼x6-inch bolts. If carriage bolts are used, you'll need 10 or more washers to make nut accessible for tightening.

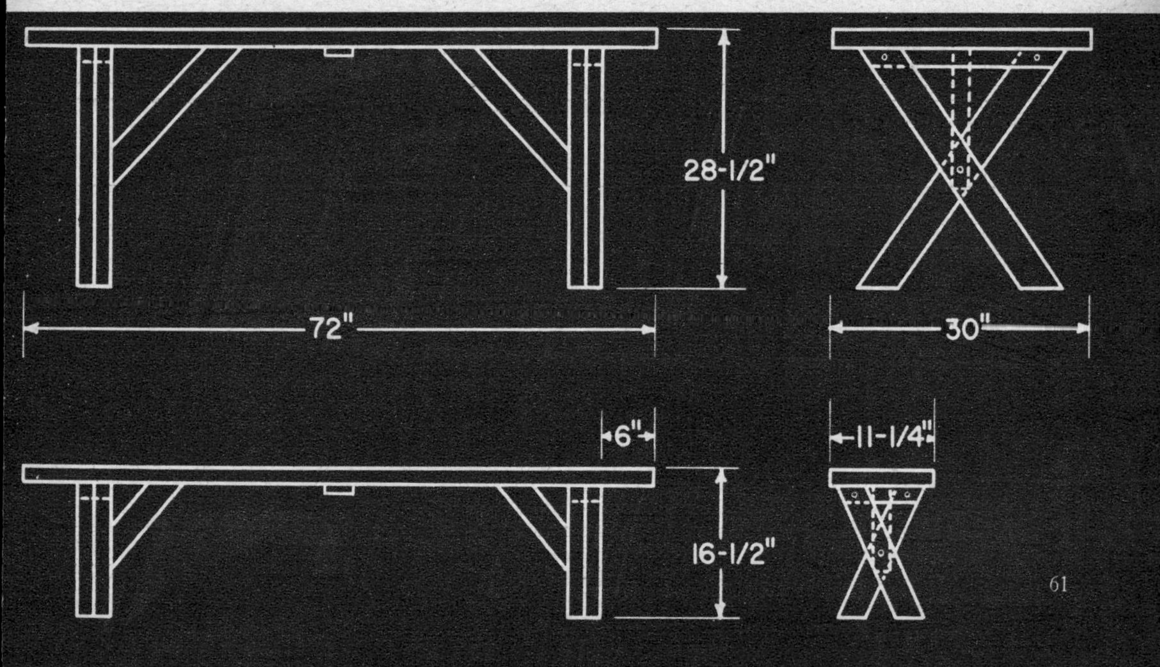

CONSTRUCT TABLE of redwood, cypress, or cedar. It provides handy serving surface, shade from sun.

TREE TABLE

It makes an ideal shaded dining area

By David X. Manners

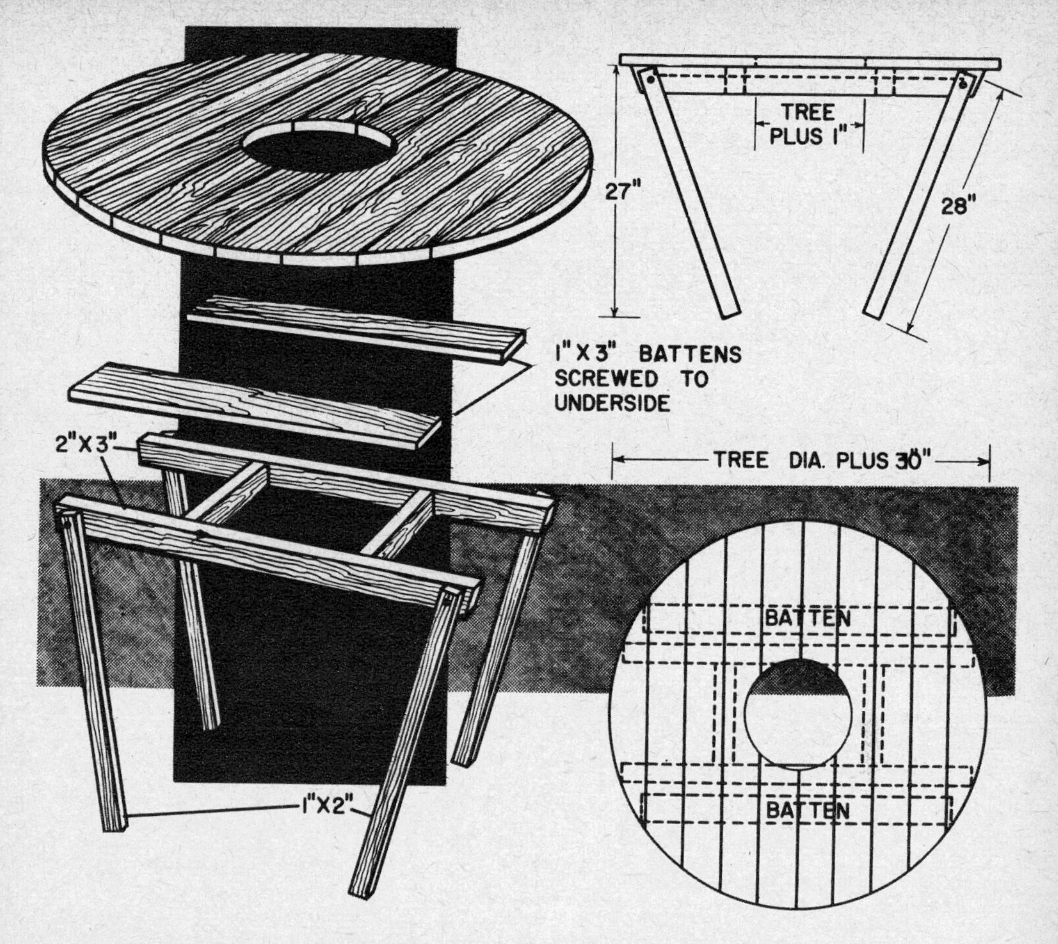

A TREE table is a perfect dining spot for small fry or a buffet-in-the-round.

A tree six inches or more in diameter is best. The inside cutout of the table should clear the trunk by about ½ inch, and the table surface should extend another 15 inches, making a diameter of 36 inches just about right for a six-inch tree. In construction, use redwood, cypress or cedar for durability, and galvanized nails. Stock 5/4 inch thick makes a really sturdy table, but ¾-inch boards serve satisfactorily.

With a pencil tied to a string, on paper or other flat surface draw a circle of the desired table size, then use the pattern for determining the length and best arrangement of the various slats. Slats can be the same or random width.

Allow about ⅛-inch space between slats. Through these spaces you will be able to follow the circle pattern below, and transfer it to the boards. Number the boards before removing them for sawing.

Make the support for the table top of 2x3 stock, bevel-cutting the ends of the two main supports so that the table top will overlap them by ½ inch. Two crosspieces are cut to the exact diameter of the tree and placed so they clear the trunk by one inch.

Nail the first crosspiece solidly in place, then set the support assembly around the tree at the desired height—27 to 28 inches is usually best—and nail to the tree. Use a level to verify that your table will be perfectly horizontal. Now nail the second crosspiece in place.

Brace the support with your knee while nailing on the table slats. Drive home one or two 7-penny galvanized box nails where boards cross each support.

Two 1x3 battens are needed under the table between the supports and the table's outside edge. Place the battens atop the table and mark locations for screws. Predrill the screwholes and then attach the battens to the table's underside.

Complete the assembly with a pair of angled 1x2 legs screwed to the ends of the table supports. The bottoms of the legs need not be nailed to the tree. Sand smooth, apply a coat of redwood sealer. •

SELECT TREE at least six inches in diameter. Folding rule used as caliper measures tree's thickness.

DRAW OUTLINE of table top, space out boards for assembly. Center cutout should clear tree ½ inch.

TRANSFER PATTERN to boards, cut curve with bandsaw or compass saw. Round off, sand edges.

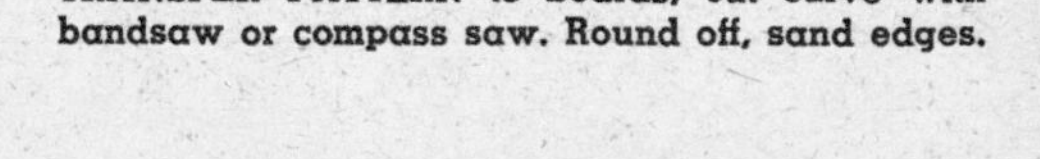

TABLE SUPPORT (cut from 2x3's) is nailed to tree 27 inches from ground. Level support before nailing.

THEN ATTACH the second crosspiece. This should clear the tree trunk by one inch on either side.

BATTENS ARE screwed to table underside. Easiest way to make holes for drilling: put batten on table.

BRACING SUPPORT with knee, attach boards forming table top. Use 7-penny galvanized box nails.

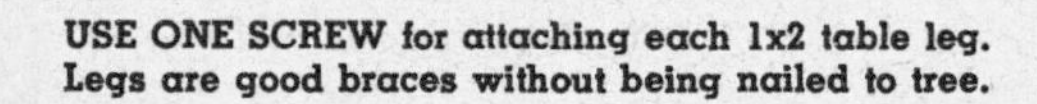

USE ONE SCREW for attaching each 1x2 table leg. Legs are good braces without being nailed to tree.

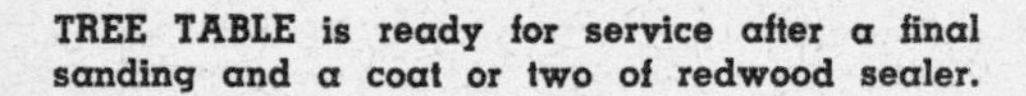

TREE TABLE is ready for service after a final sanding and a coat or two of redwood sealer.

LAWN CHAIRS

These can be made easily from any kind of scrap lumber

By David X. Manners

SPECIALLY DESIGNED for comfort, these lawn chairs are simple to build. Once the pattern has been established, additional chairs take only about half an hour to build. Chairs are ideal for lawn, porch or terrace.

LAWN chairs require many short pieces of wood, and are an ideal project for turning scrap around the home or shop to handsome use. Any type of ¾-inch boards will do—shelving, tongue-and-groove stock, even crating lumber. To do it right, though, plan to build at least three of the chairs at a clip.

It works this way: Once the pattern is established, chair-building goes fast. It takes about two hours to build one chair —but only *half an hour* for every chair after that. You can easily build three or four in a morning. So tool up for mass production.

First step, cut out the sidepieces that form the seat support and rear legs. On a board at least 1x8x26 inches, mark off a grid of three-inch squares. With the grid as a guide, draw the leg pattern, following the design shown in the sketch. Each large square on the board is the equivalent of a small square in the sketch, so transcribe the pattern square for square.

Cut out the sidepiece, as marked, with bandsaw or keyhole saw. You can even hack it out on a tablesaw or with a portable power saw. Smooth the edges of the sidepiece with rasp, surform file or plane, and then sand. Using the sidepiece you have cut as a pattern, mark the sidepieces for all the other chairs you are building, and cut them.

Templates Recommended

Next, mark the pattern for a front leg on a 1x5x21-inch board. Cut out the leg and smooth. Use it as template for cutting out all the other legs you'll need and add them to your stockpile. You can vary the curves or pattern of the leg to suit your own taste or fancy, adding whatever embellishments you like.

For each chair you plan to build, cut four pieces 1x4x20½-inch seat boards (more pieces if you use narrower stock), a 1x1¾-inch arm support, a 1x4½x17¼-inch leg spreader, a 1x5⅜x25-inch front-

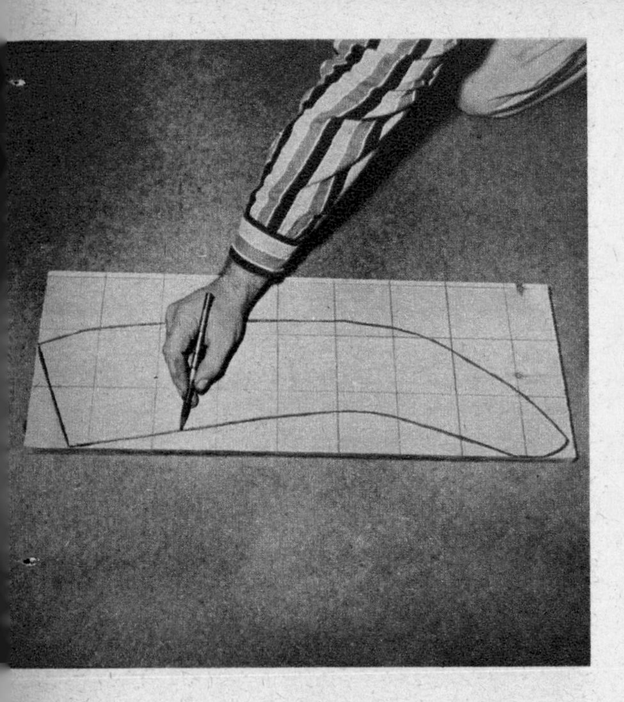

MARK OFF three-inch squares on board. Squares make it easy to transcribe pattern of sidepieces.

piece, a 1x1¼x25-inch finishing strip. This completes cutting except for back boards. Back boards are preferably cut after first chair base is assembled, so that a test fitting can be made.

You can use either 8-penny finishing nails or No. 6 flathead wood screws 1½ inches long for all assembly operations, or a combination of both, but always use screws at points where strength is needed.

Start assembly by attaching a sidepiece to the inside edge of a front leg at a point eight inches from bottom. Check with a try square to be sure attachment of leg is perpendicular.

Join a pair of assembled sidepieces and legs with a frontpiece, placed so its top edge is flush with top edge of sidepiece. Attach seat boards allowing ¾ inch overlap at each side and about ¼ inch between boards. A narrow finishing strip at front completes the seat. Notch the finishing strip on each side, as required, where it meets the upper part of the leg.

Attach arms to rear support, using screws. Chair back may now be attached to this support.

Chair backs may be made with 3, 4, or 5 boards, depending on board width and their spacing. Design and curve of these

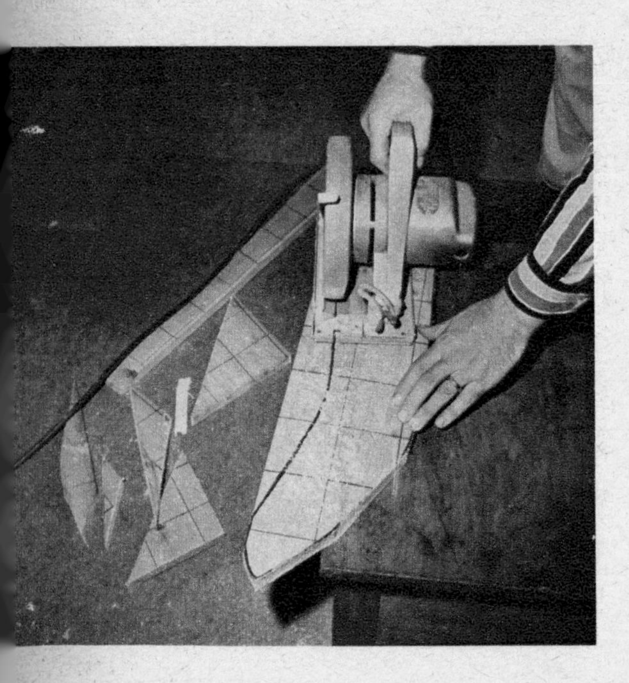

CUT OUT pattern on bandsaw or with keyhole saw. Or cut it with power saw by making series of cuts.

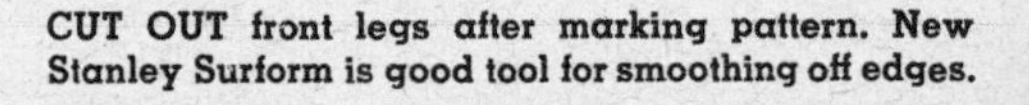

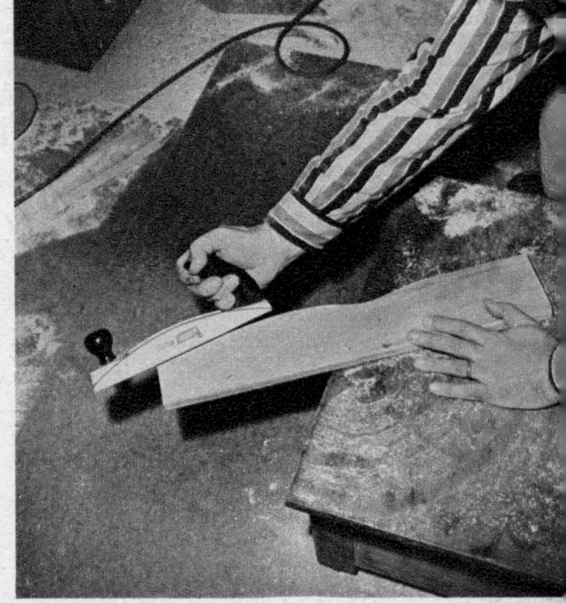

CUT OUT front legs after marking pattern. New Stanley Surform is good tool for smoothing off edges.

ATTACH sidepieces to inside edge of front legs with nails or wood screws. Try-square checks legs for plumbness. Diagrams below give measurements needed to build lawn chairs. Follow them carefully.

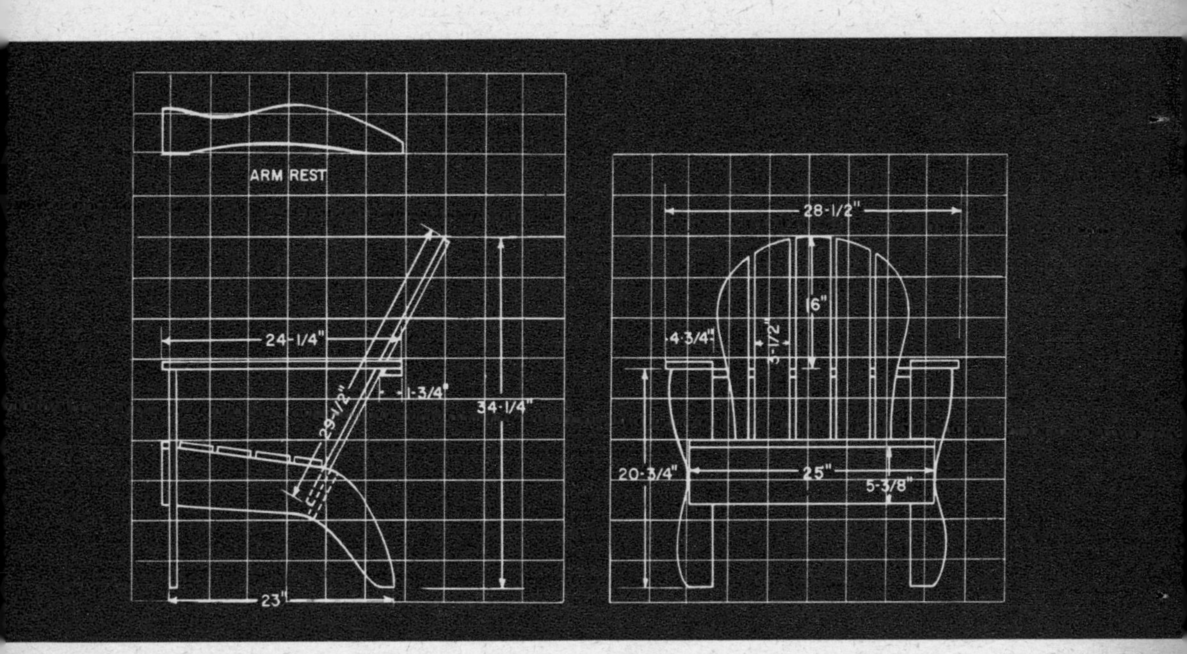

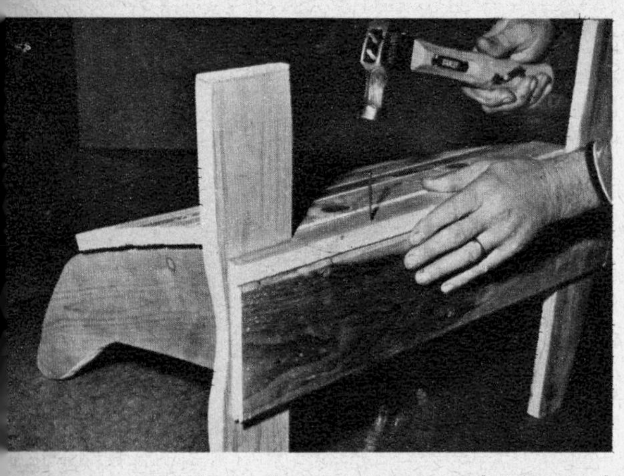

ATTACH cross board to tie legs together, then nail seat boards to sidepieces, allowing ¾-inch overlap.

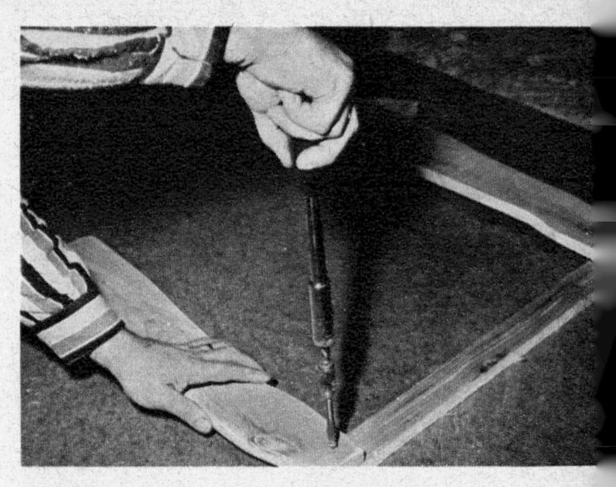

ATTACH arms to back support, front legs with screws. Countersink slightly, fill in with wood putty.

ONCE pattern of back curvature is determined, cut pair of outside boards for each chair back.

boards can be largely of your own choosing, or you can closely follow the pattern shown. A power drum sander is especially useful in sculpturing pleasing shapes.

Attach back boards to arm support so that high point of back measures at least 16 inches above support. This means that center board of back must be at least 27½ inches long. Outside boards are about 2 inches shorter at their highest point.

Back is firmly secured to chair base with a spreader piece positioned to hold boards firmly against back of seat. Board ends are attached to spreader. Attach chair arms to front legs with screws.

Finish chairs with two coats of an outdoor enamel such as Dulux Trim & Shutter paint, following manufacturer's instructions on the can. •

DRUM SANDER makes it easy to sculpture attractive shapes. Round off edges of every board.

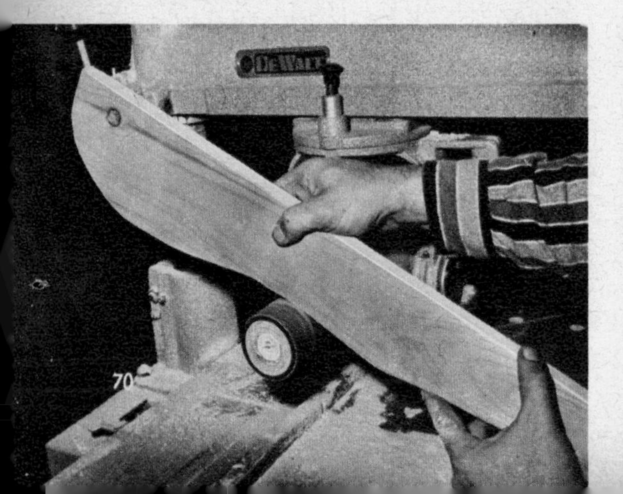

ATTACH back boards to arm support so that high point of back is at least 16 inches above support.

SPREADER BOARD holds ends of back boards firmly against seat. Screw or nail in place. Screw or nail back boards to spreader. Final result will be chairs shown in photo left. Since these chairs are easy to build, make several of them.

CORD LOUNGE

Handsome Redwood and plastic cord blend together for lawn luxury

By Darrell Huff and Paul Corey

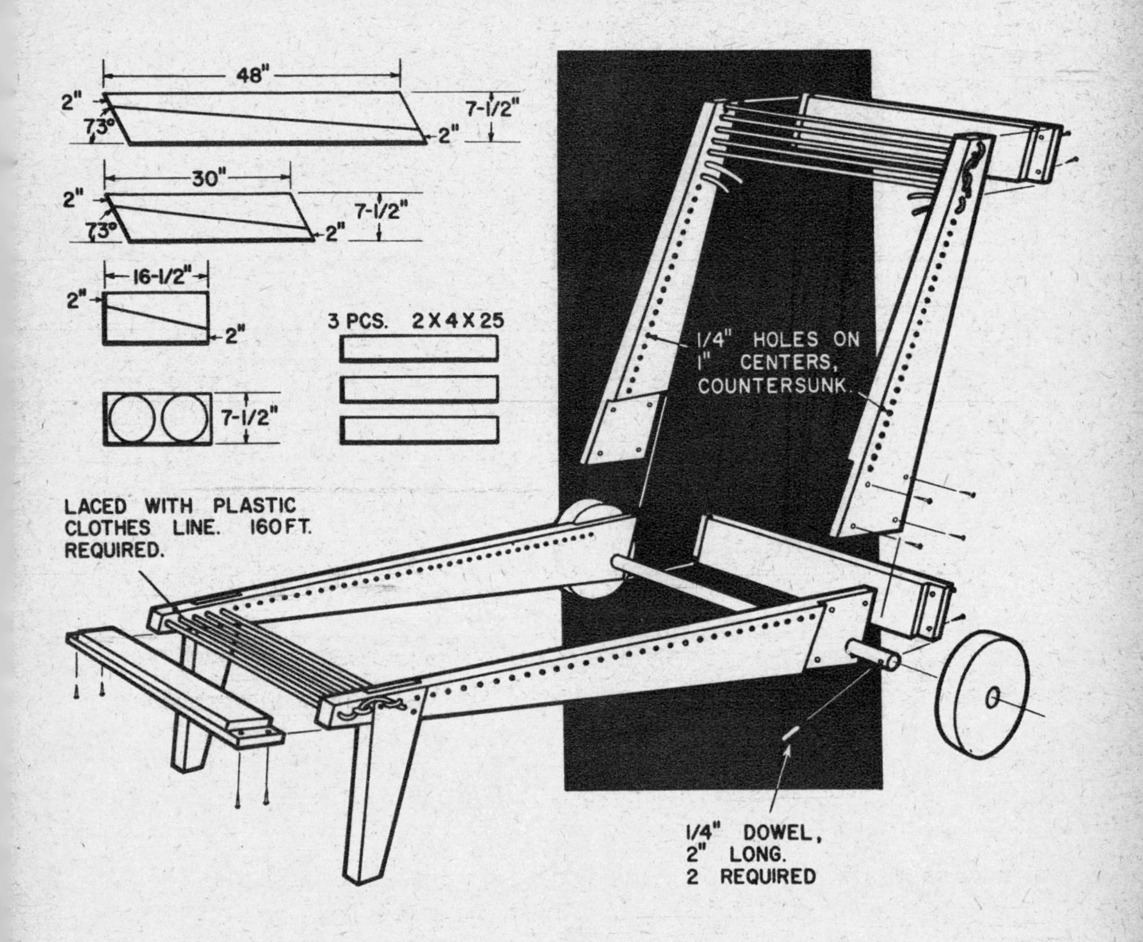

REDWOOD is the logical material for this handsome lawn piece, which is designed to use standard dimension lumber. You'll need a 10-foot length of 2x8 and 75 inches of 2x4. You'll also need 31 inches of one-inch dowel and four inches of ¼-inch dowel.

String this lounge with 160 feet of plastic cord or clothesline. Hardware needed includes 12 2½-inch No. 12 and 12 1½-inch No. 8 wood screws, chrome plated or flathead galvanized.

Pad used with it is the standard 24 x 74-inch kind sold by furniture stores and mail-order houses. Photos on these pages show lounge with and without pad. It can be used either way. Green is a good choice in pad color because it contrasts nicely with the redwood and white plastic cord. •

FROM 10-foot length of 2x8 (or lumber 1⅝ inches thick, 7½ inches wide) cut a 16½-inch length. Set miter gauge at 73 degrees, cut off one 48-inch and one 30-inch length. Save rest of 2x8 for wheels.

MARK points 2 inches from the acute angles on the 48 and 30-inch pieces of 2x8, and taper-rip between these points. Mark them "seat" and "back" as shown. Then taper-rip 16-inch 2x8 boards.

PLACE "seat" and "back" pieces together and mark them for making half-lap joints. For marking, one "seat" is on top of "back," other is vice versa.

COMPLETE the joints just marked by cutting out stock to the line. Depth of cut should be exactly half the thickness of the lumber, as shown below.

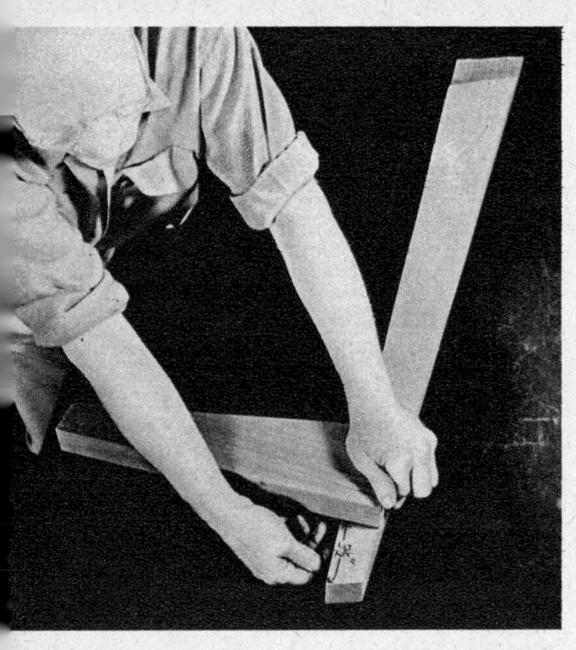

LAY OUT a "seat" piece joint side up. Place leg on it, 3½ inches from tip. Make two lines on "seat," one on leg for lap joints. Repeat with other "seat" and leg. Remove stock to make necessary joints.

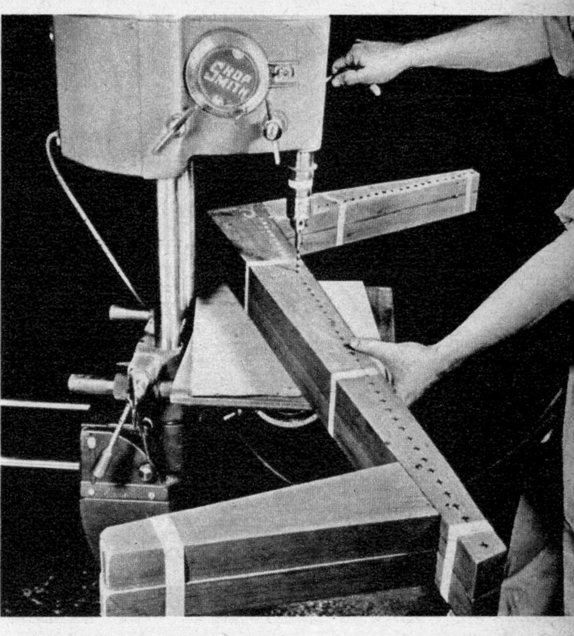

ASSEMBLE each set of three pieces. Draw lines one inch from taper-cut side along "seat," "back." Tape assemblies together. Drill ¼-inch holes at one-inch intervals along "back" and "seat."

MEASURE 1½ inches from each edge where "seat," "back" join. With this point as center, drill one-inch hole through assemblies. Remove tape, ream out all the ¼-inch cord holes slightly with a countersink so that they look like the ones shown in this picture. Plastic cord will fit through these holes later on.

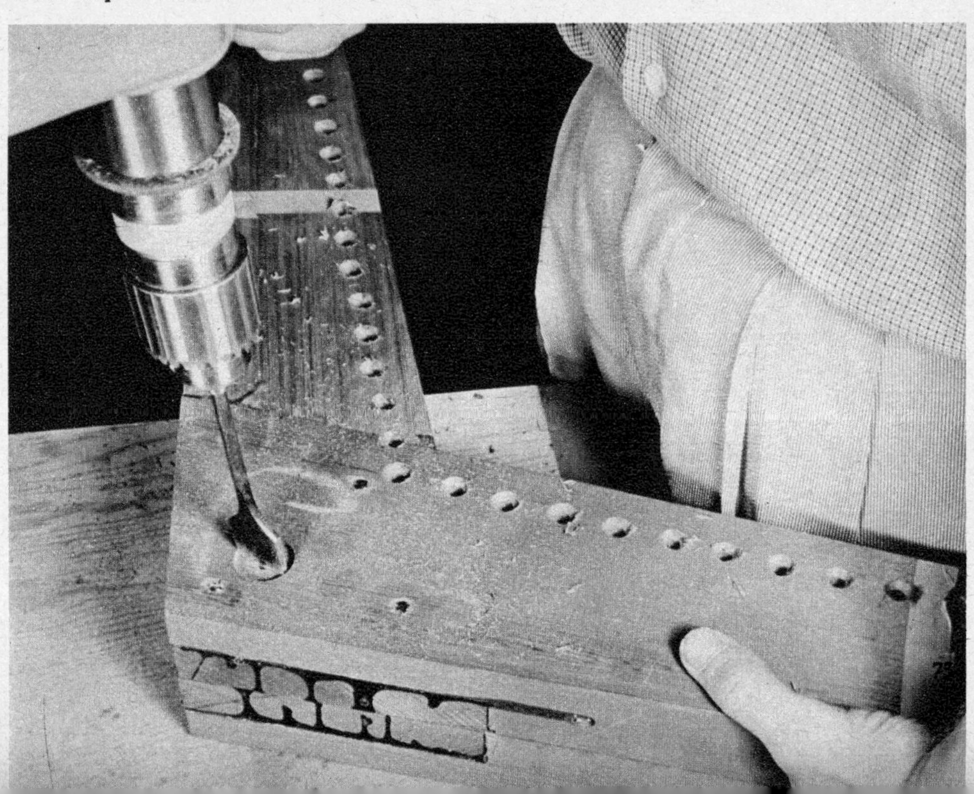

RABBET both ends of each of three pieces of 2x4. Make rabbets half the thickness of 2x4 and as wide as the 2x8 lumber is thick. Bevel the edge of one of pieces, using setting of 3 degrees, trim slightly.

COMPLETE assembly. With glue and screws, fasten on two unbeveled pieces. Fasten on beveled stretcher just in front of legs, so that beveled edge bears neatly against front edges of legs.

CUT OUT pair of wheels, making them as large as your 2x8 lumber permits. Cut them on jig saw or band saw, or rough them out on circular saw, sand them to shape. Drill one-inch hole in wheels.

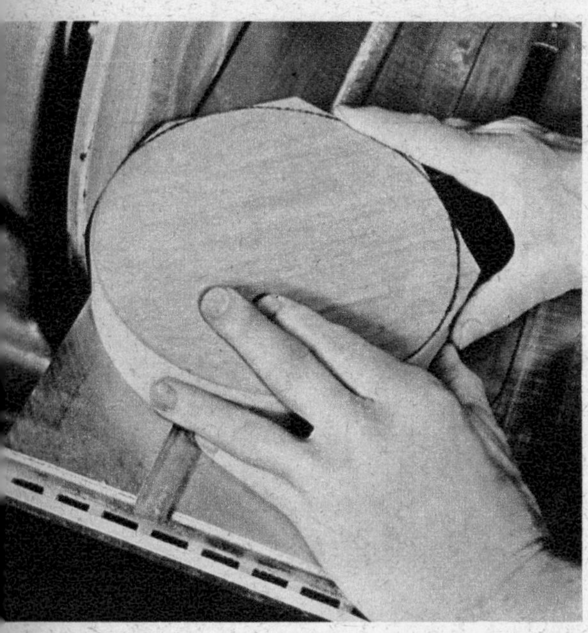

CUT OUT piece of one-inch dowel to 31-inch length. Drill a 1/4-inch hole through the dowel 1/2 inch from each end. This serves as axle for wheels. Then cut two two-inch lengths of 1/4-inch dowel as axle pins.

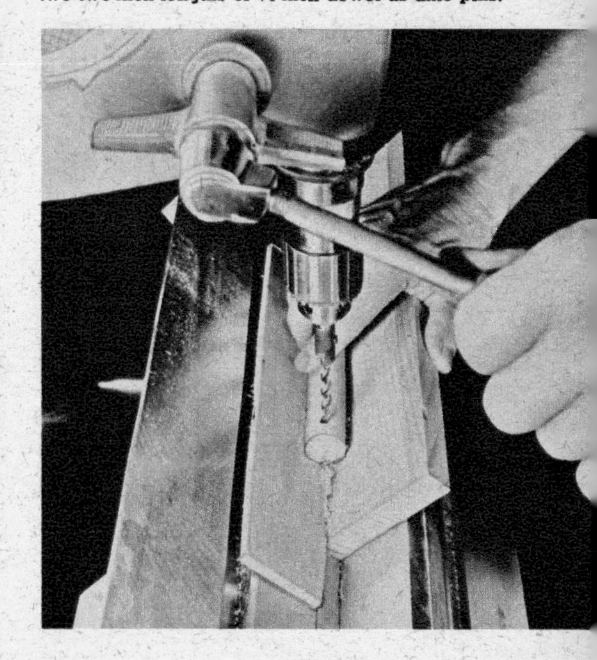

SAND chaise smooth and apply the finish to frame, axle and wheels. Two coats of varnish will do the job, but be sure to use a type recommended for outdoor furniture. Then slip axle through holes in chaise, put on wheels, and secure by driving in the small pins you have made from ¼-inch dowel. Next step in constructing the cord lounge is to weave the plastic cord or clothesline into place on the frame.

WEAVE in plastic cord. Do not make it very tight as you go. Then work from the middle toward the ends, taking up slack. Do this several times and the cord will be as tight as you wish.

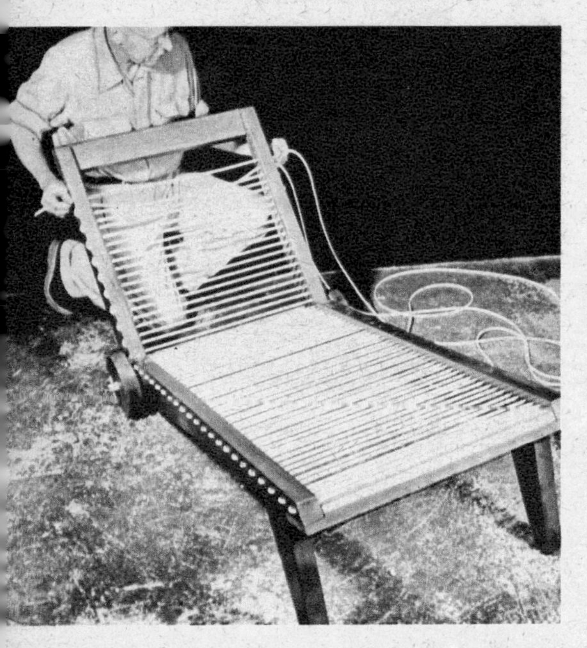

SECURE both ends of the plastic cord by slipping under two loops, like this. This picture also shows how to tighten the cord. Cord lounge should now be in good shape, ready for use in your back yard.

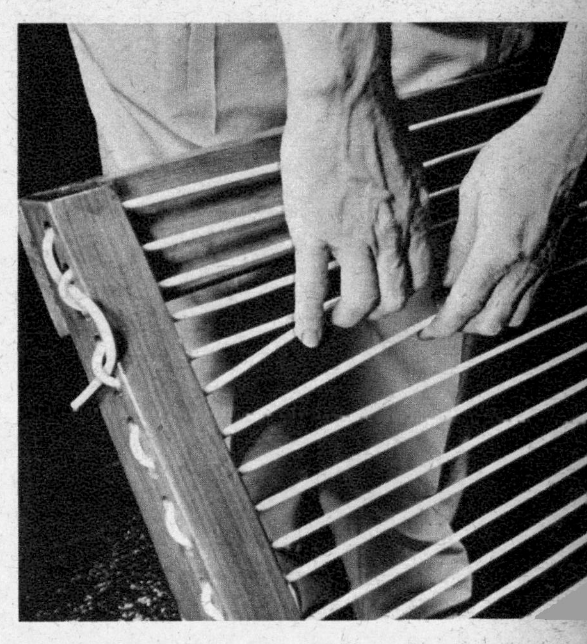

CHAISE LONGUE

Its contours substitute for upholstery and make for comfortable lounging

By Bill Baker

FOLLOWING GRAPH BELOW, make layout of chaise longue side pieces on heavy paper. Transfer pattern to piece of Duraply, then cut out side pieces.

TACK SIDES together temporarily, then sand inside curves with a drum sander. Outside curves and long edges are sanded with portable belt sander.

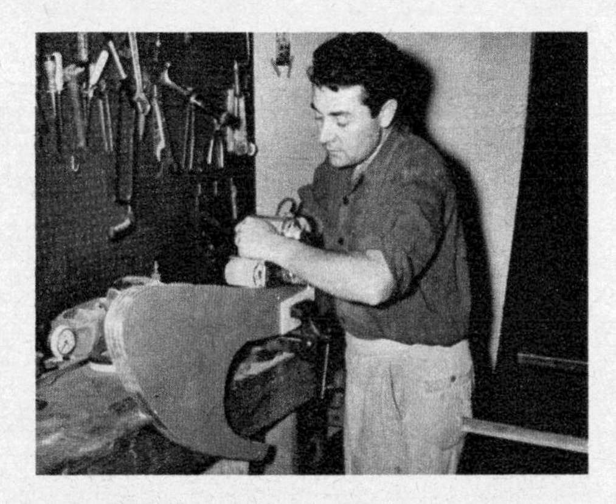

WITH SANDING completed and both pieces stili tacked together, the side pattern is replaced again and the hole for the wheel axle is carefully marked.

USING FULL-SIZE PATTERN, mark location of back supports on side pieces. Then mount supports with weldwood glue, 1¼-inch No. 12 flathead screws.

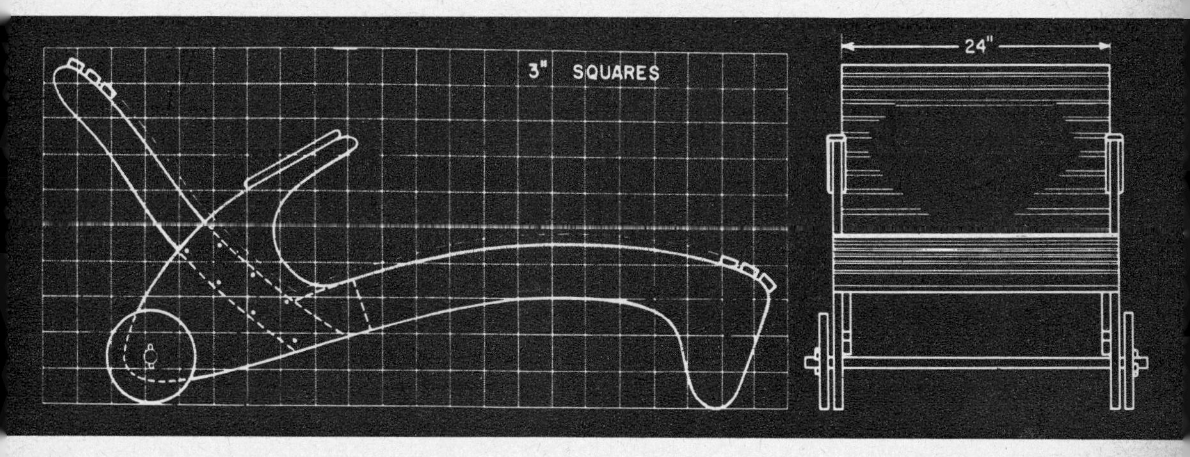

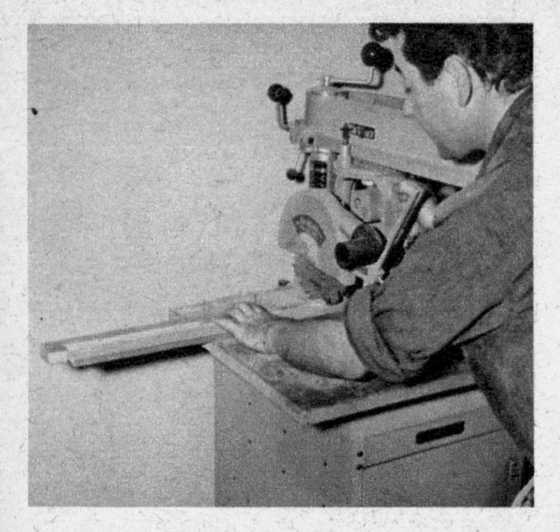

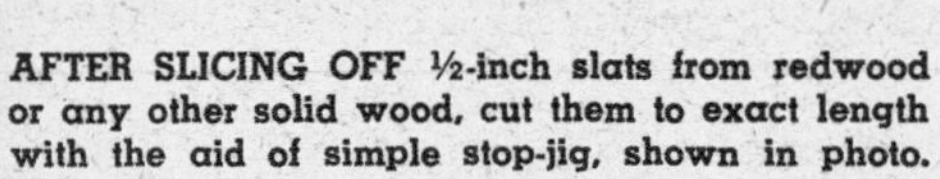

AFTER SLICING OFF ½-inch slats from redwood or any other solid wood, cut them to exact length with the aid of simple stop-jig, shown in photo.

WITH SLATS properly bored on each end, and the edges beveled, mount back axle in holes. Then nail top slat of back and front slat of seat in place.

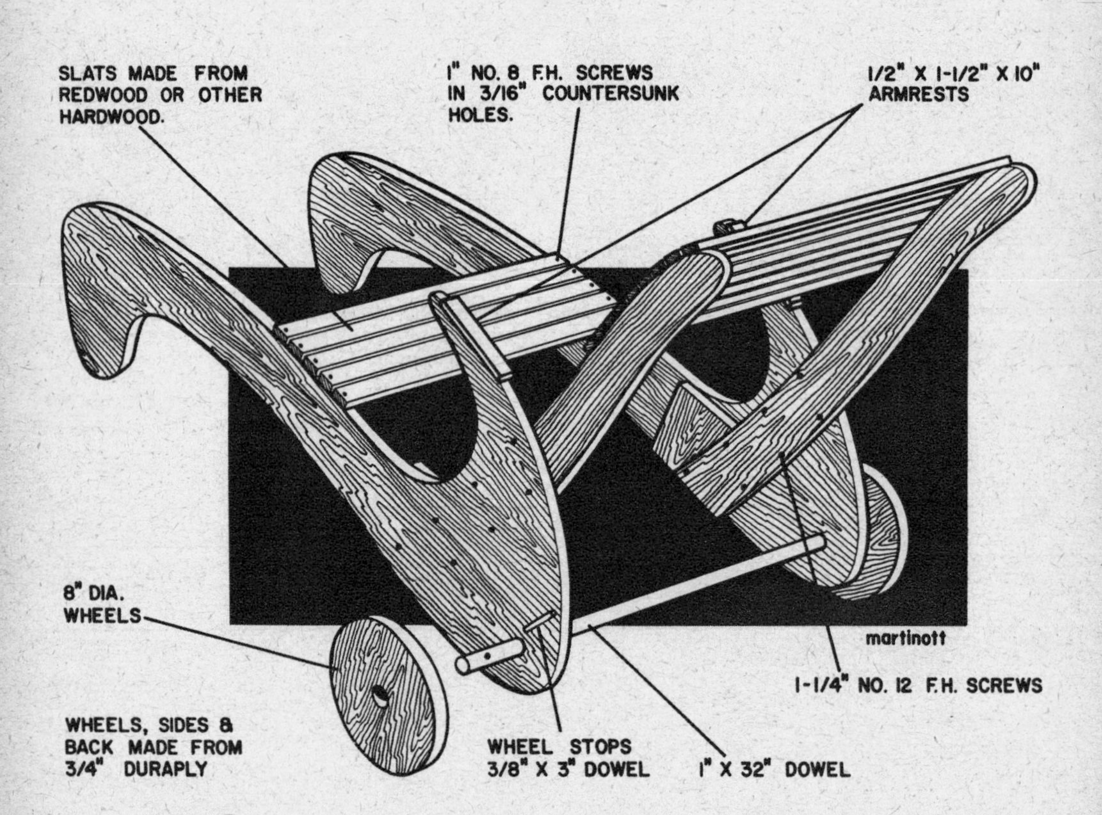

STARTING FROM the very back, nail the seat slats ¼ inch apart. Use a ¼-inch spacer to get the correct spacing. Use 3D finish nails near screwhole.

AFTER ALL the seat slats are properly nailed in place, bore ⅛-inch pilot holes into the Duraply edges, as shown in the photo directly to the left.

THEN INSERT No. 8 or No. 9 flathead screws in the 3/16-inch countersunk holes in each end of each slat. Screw heads should recede 1/16 of an inch.

BEYOND ROUND PART of arms, mount solid wood armrests. These measure ½ inch thick, 1½ inches wide, 10 inches long. Mount with glue and No. 8 flathead screws.

PLACE WHEEL on axle rod, hold tightly against side piece, bore ⅜-inch hole through axle. Hole should extend ⅛ inch beyond wheel for wheel stop. It'll keep wheel in place.

SAND ENTIRE unit with an electric sander (as shown) or do job by hand. Entire back and seat are sanded to give the slats the proper rounding and contour. Do neat, thorough job.

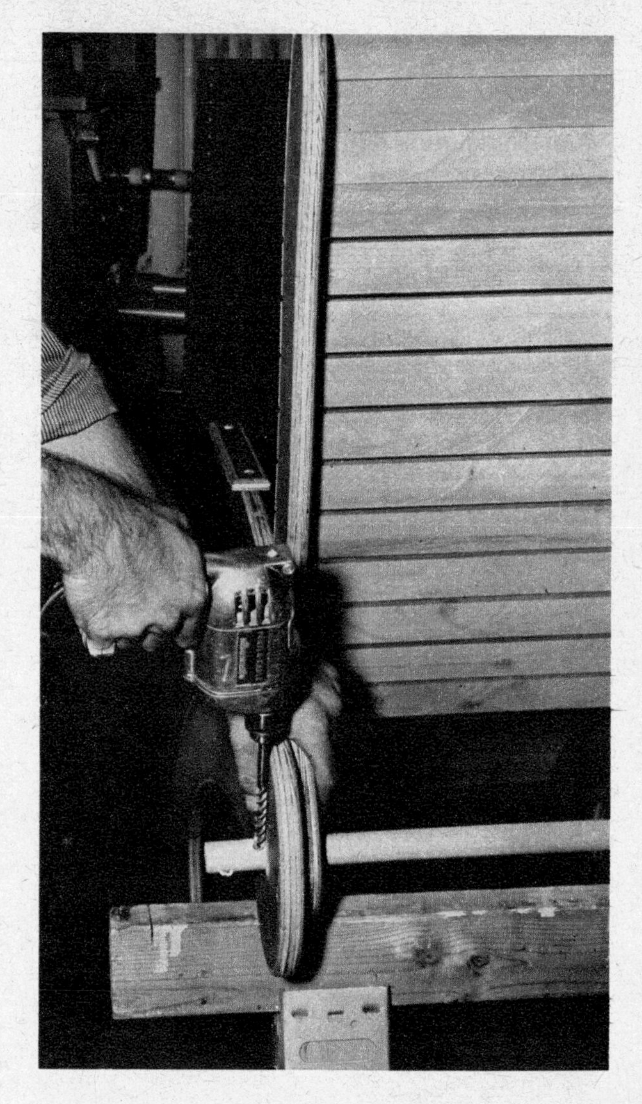

MATERIALS NEEDED:

One sheet of Duraply 3/4 inch x 4 feet x 8 feet
Solid wood for 26 slats 1/2x1 1/2x24 inches
One hardwood dowel 1 inch diameter—
36 inches long
Six inch piece hardwood dowel 3/8 inch
One dozen flathead screws 1 1/4 inches, No. 12
Five dozen flathead screws one inch, No. 9
One pound 3d finish nails
Waterproof weldwood glue
No. 1, No. 1/2 sandpaper

AFTER WHEEL STOP (about 2 1/2 or 3 inches long) has been mounted in place, main wheel axle is cut off 5/8 inch beyond wheel stop, and ends are rounded off with a hand file.

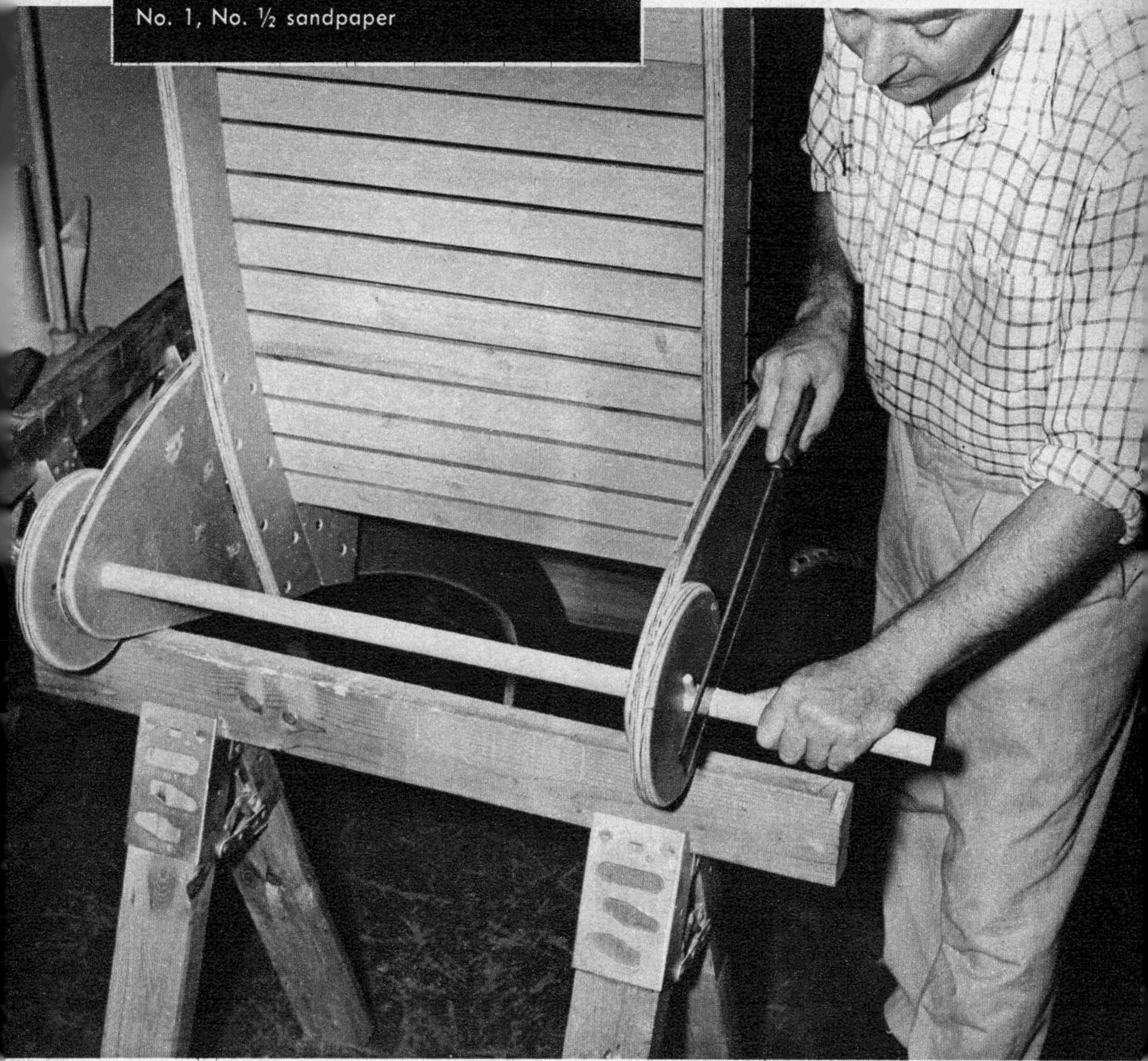

ADJUSTABLE LOUNGE

In addition to being decorative, it folds into various positions

By Bill Baker

MAKE a full size layout as shown in the graph. Then cut out pattern "A" (sides), trace same on two pieces of 2-inch x 8-inch x 6-foot solid wood. Replace pattern "A" to full size layout, tape it on and then cut out pattern "B" (sides of back), trace same onto the 2x8-inch board. Then tape back in place. Next, cut out pattern "C". Trace to same boards and replace. Now cut out pattern "J". Trace to boards and replace.

On a board of 2-inch x 10-inch x 3-feet solid wood, trace pattern "D" and "I" (legs and wheels). Next, cut out all pieces previously marked. Then temporarily tack the pairs together and sand edges smooth, and bore all holes.

Because of variation of thickness in lumber, dimensions of length of dowels as well as cross pieces are not given. Follow instructions carefully.

The width of chaise seat is 24 inches. Deduct both thicknesses of pieces "A" (sides) from 24 inches and the result will give you the length of "E" (front cross piece). Cut out one piece from 2x3-inch lumber and place it between the two "A" pieces. Hold it in place with an 8D finishing nail on each side. Next bore ¼-inch pilot holes, insert ⅜x3½-inch leg bolts with washers and tighten. Also use waterproof weldwood glue.

Hold back end in place and measure distance between both bottoms of one-inch holes in pieces "A". Cut a one-inch hardwood dowel to this length. In center of thickness of dowel bore ⅛-inch pilot holes on both ends. Place dowel in holes, insert a 2-inch No. 14 roundhead screw with washer on both outsides of "A" and tighten. Plane excess of front piece "E" off and sand.

Notch upper outside of both legs "D" and mount same on inside of sides "A" 5½ inches from front. See diagrams. Use waterproof weldwood glue only on one leg. Next measure again distance between both bottoms of one-inch holes, as done previously. Cut one-inch dowel to length, bore pilot holes on each end, and mount between legs "D" by first taking off unglued leg and finally mounting back in position with dowel, using glue. For legs as well as both ends of dowel use 2-inch No. 14 roundhead screws with washers.

Bore two ¼-inch holes in each piece "J" (wheel axle support) as shown in diagram. Glue and screw both pieces onto bottom edge of both "A", 10½ inches from back end, using 2-inch No. 14 roundhead screws and washers.

Cut a one-inch dowel 29 inches long. Sand six inches on each end well and round off ends. On sanded places rub large amount of paraffin. Now insert dowel in one-inch holes of "J" (wheel axle supports) leaving equal amount extended on each end.

Slide wheels on axle leaving about ⅛-inch play between them and "A" (sides). Now make a mark at outside surface of wheels on axle. Remove wheels and bore ¼-inch holes through axle about ⅛ inch toward outsides from previous marks. Mount wheels again in position and glue ¼-inch hardwood dowels 2½ inches long in holes, leaving equal amount extended out on both ends. See identification drawing on print.

For rope handle of chaise bore two ½-inch holes 8 inches apart in center of "E" (front cross piece).

MAKE FULL-SIZE layout of parts according to graph. Cut out patterns, transfer to 2x8-inch boards.

PLACE PARTS in pairs, sand edges. Bore all holes (according to diagram) except shorter depth holes.

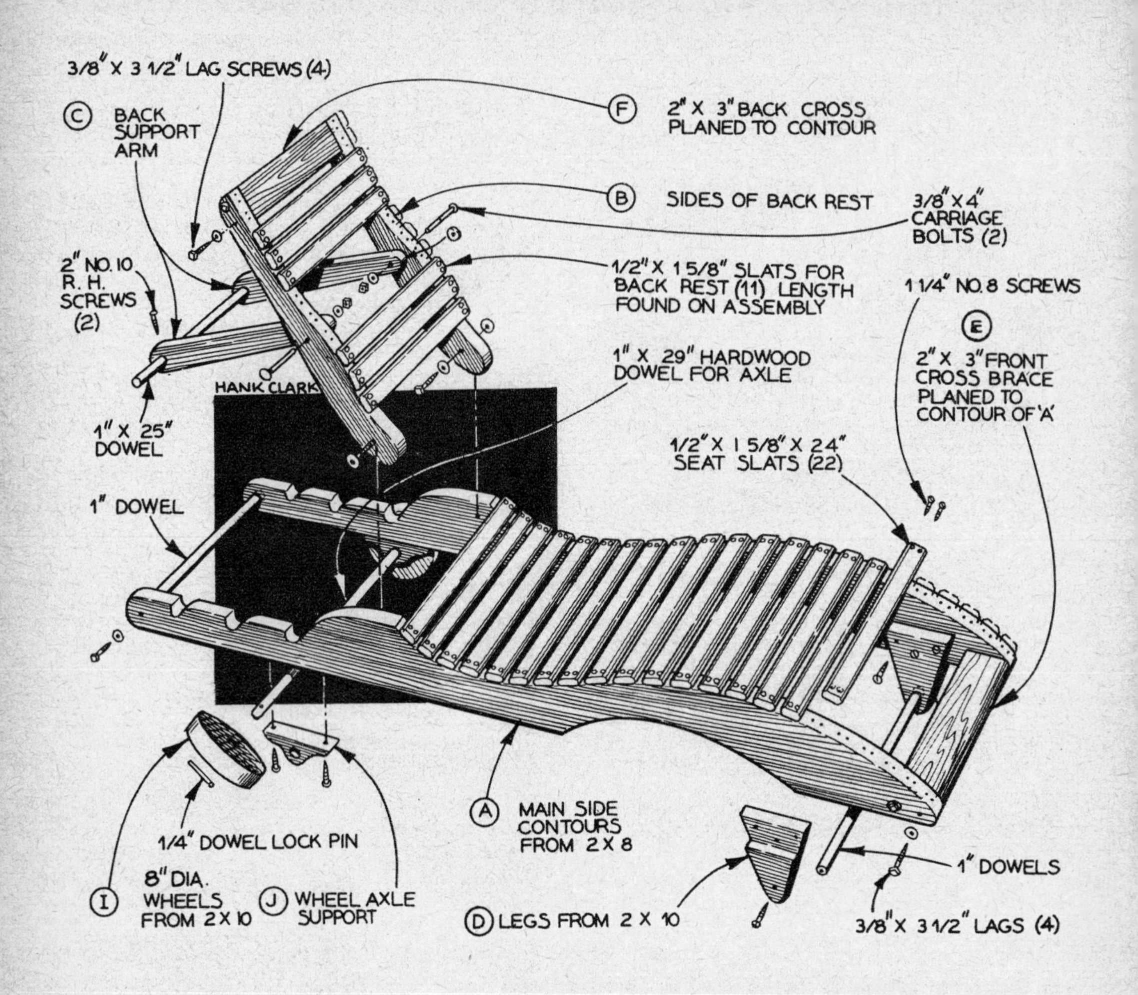

MATERIALS NEEDED:

- 2 boards—2 inch thick x 8 inch wide x 6 feet long
- 1 board—2 inch thick x 10 inch wide x 3 feet long
- 1 board—2 inch thick x 3 inches wide x 4 feet long
- 6 boards—½ inch thick x 2 inches wide (1⅝ net) x 12 feet long
- 4 lengths (usually 3 feet each) 1 inch hardwood dowel
- 1 length of 5 inches ¼-inch hardwood dowel
- 4 pieces carriage bolts ⅜ inch x 4 inches with washers
- 8 pieces leg bolts ⅜ inch x 3½ inches with washers
- 4 pieces—½ inch washers
- 14 pieces roundhead screws—2 inch No. 14
- 2 pieces roundhead screws—2 inch No. 10
- 1 gross flathead screws—1¼ inch No. 8
- ¼ pound brads—1 inch, No. 18
- Few 8-d finishing nails
- 18 inch length of ⅜ inch rope
- Waterproof weldwood glue
- Sandpaper No. 1 and No. ½
- 1 cake of paraffin

Note: If redwood is used, it is advisable to use brass screws. When painted with redwood oil or stain, follow instructions of manufacturer.

Full-size templates are available for this project. They may be had by sending $1.00 to Bill Baker, Fawcett Publications, P. O. Box 331, GPO, New York 1, New York

Measure inside clearance of chaise. From this dimension deduct the total thickness of both pieces "B" (sides of back rest) and also deduct ¼ inch for clearance. The final result is the length of piece "F" (back cross piece). Cut one piece out of 2x3-inch wood and place it between both pieces "B," holding it in place with 8D finishing nails. See diagram. Next proceed identically as previously done with front cross piece "E". Plane excess off and sand smooth.

Mount back rest in bottom part of chaise bolting it on with ¾x4-inch carriage bolts with ⅜-inch washer on inside of "B" only. When inserting bolts slide a ½-inch washer between "A" and "B" pieces on each side.

Cut a one-inch dowel 25 inches long and sand well. Insert same through one-inch holes of pieces "C" (back supports) leaving about four inches extended out on each end. Next mount this assembly between both pieces "B" (sides of back rest), bolting it with ⅜x4-inch carriage bolts using ⅜-inch washers on inside only where nuts are. When inserting bolts mount ½-inch washer between "B" and "C" on both sides. Now straighten pieces "C" out, bore $\frac{3}{16}$-inch holes through them to dowel. Insert 2-inch No. 10 roundhead screws with washers and tighten.

Cut 22 pieces of slate ½ inch thick x 1⅝ inches wide x 24 inches long (net dimension) for seat of chaise. Set back up straight into first notch. Make a mark two inches from front edge of "B" on top edges of "A." This is where the last slat should mount. For the placing of the first one see diagram.

Cut 11 slats for back. The length of them is determined by the width of chaise back.

Bore one $\frac{3}{16}$-inch hole ⅝ inch from each end of each slat. Countersink so that flatheads will recede $\frac{1}{16}$ inch. Next chamfer all four edges and the two ends on the outside surface.

Near the hole on each end of slats start a one-inch No. 18 brad. Temporarily start first slat in front of seat, then last slat as marked before. Make yourself a spacer strip ½ inch thick and 25 inches long. With help of same, start tacking all other slats in between. Keep moving them until spaces are approximately even. Now with back still upright proceed as done previously, starting with top slat making sure that bottom slat is clear of adjoining slat of seat. Once all slats are in place nail brads all the way in and countersink them. Next drill ⅛-inch pilot holes, then insert 1¼-inch No. 8 flathead screws and tighten. Sand all sharp edges and make sure all screwheads are set below surface.

After chaise is painted, cut a piece of rope ⅜-inch thick and insert in holes of front piece "E", leaving enough slack to serve as handle, then secure with knots in back. •

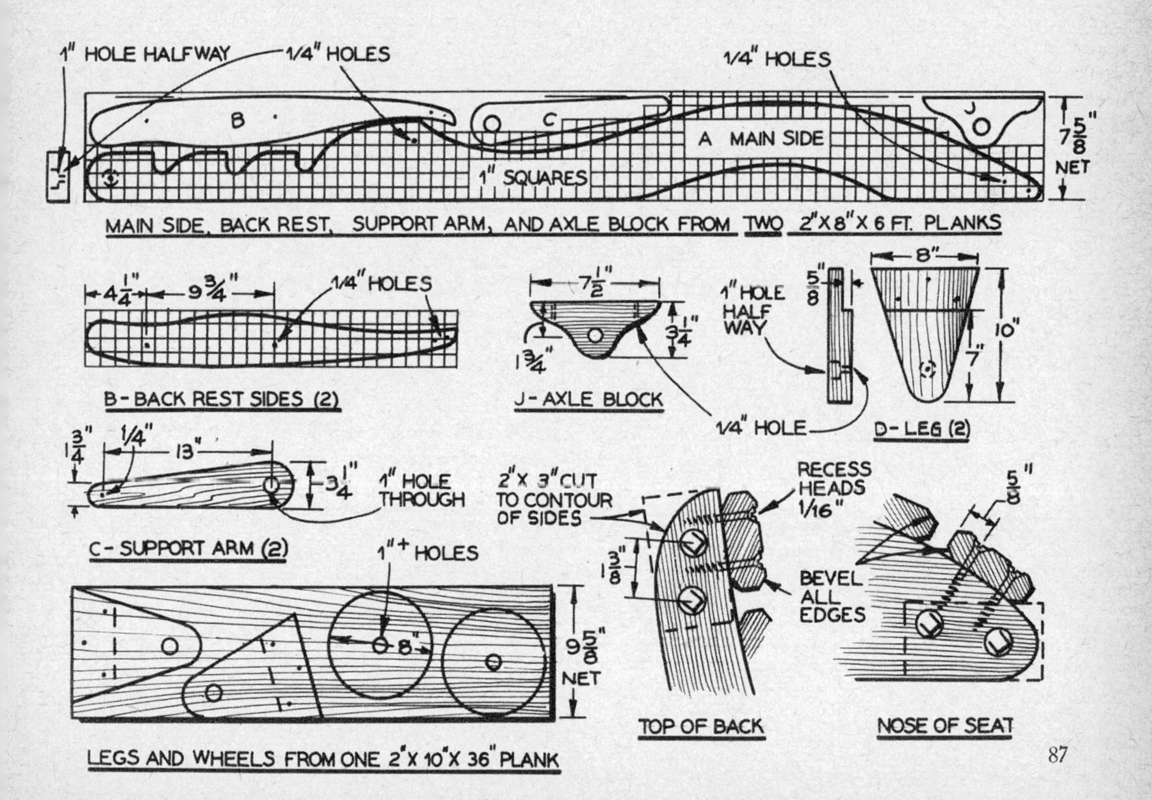

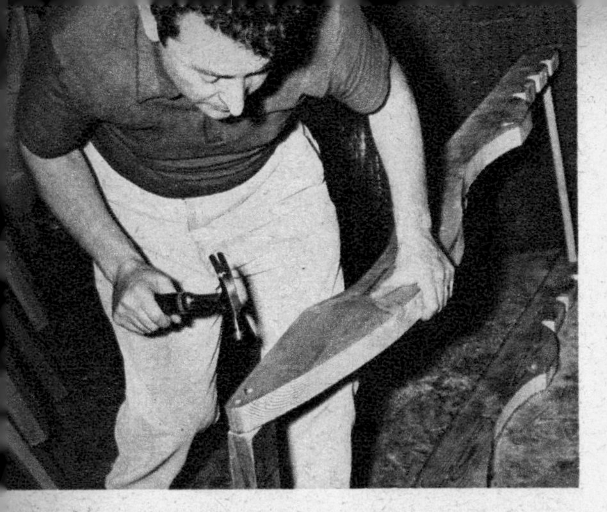

MOUNT front cross piece between sides with 8D finishing nails between the two holes. Keep flush.

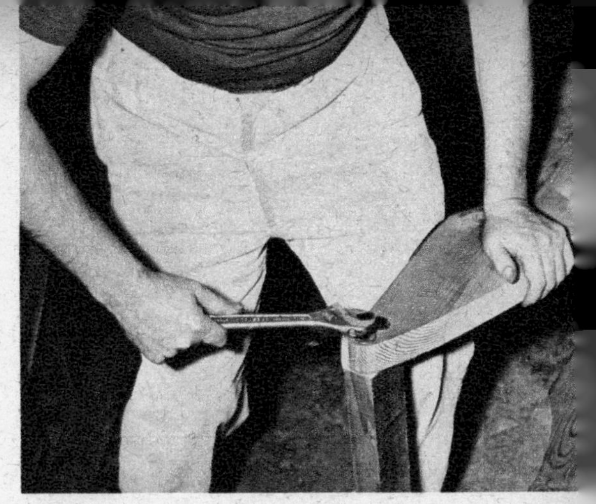

INSERT LEG BOLTS (⅜x3½-inch) with washers; ¼-inch pilot holes are bored in cross pieces first.

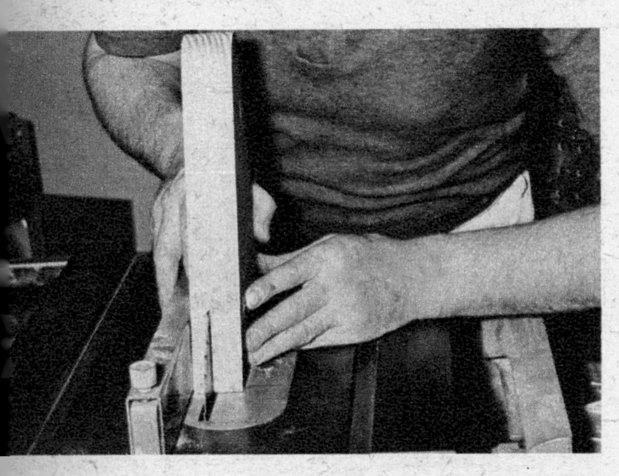

NOTCH LEGS. Table saw is used to full depth. Finish with hand saw, use table saw for cross cutting.

AFTER ONE LEG is mounted, other leg is inserted with dowel axle, then glued and fastened in place.

CROSS PIECES are planed flush with contour of the sides. Use a hand plane for this simple operation.

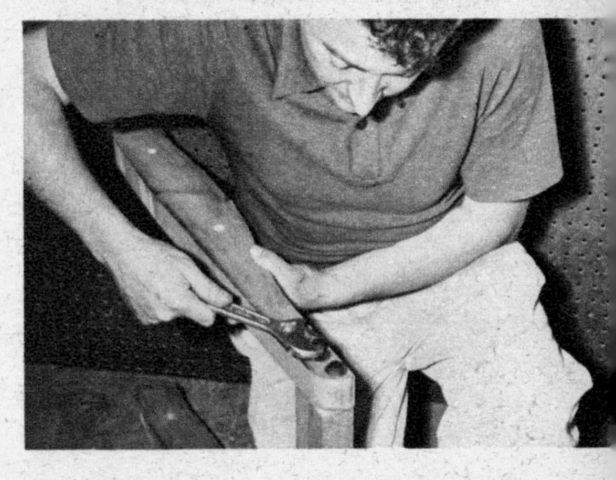

TOP CROSS PIECE is mounted between sides of back rest with leg bolts. Keep all parts flush.

WHEEL AXLE supports are mounted next to bottom edge of each side piece, flush with outside surfaces.

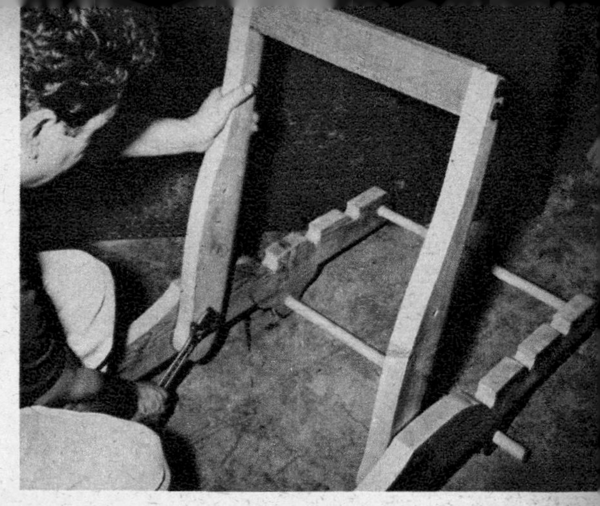

BACK REST is mounted between the sides with ½-inch washer between them for clearance.

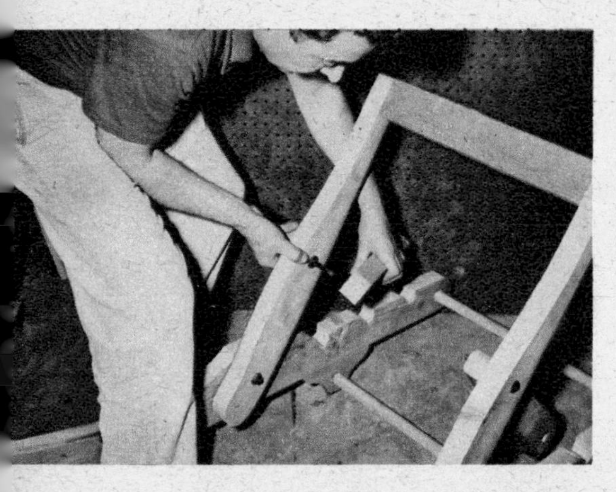

BACK SUPPORTS are mounted next to inside of the sides of the back rest, with ½-inch washer between.

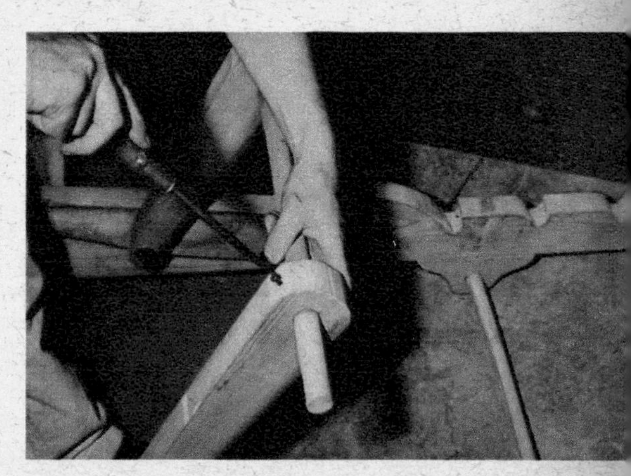

INSERT 1-inch dowel through holes of back supports. Leave equal overlap and fasten dowel.

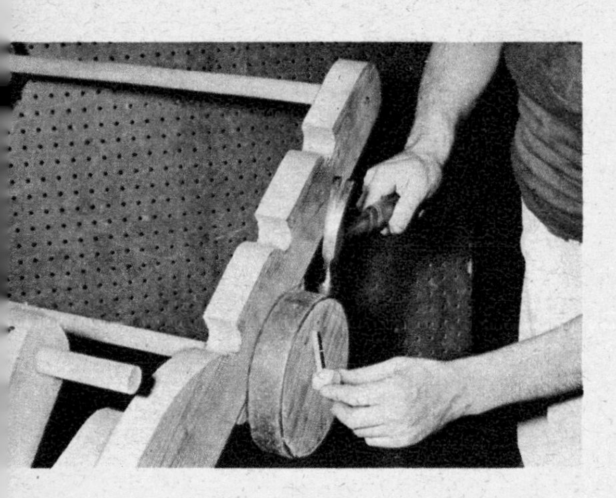

MOUNT WHEELS, insert ¼x2-inch wheel stop (dowel) through axle; allow ⅛-inch clearance.

WITH BACK REST in upright position, seat slats are mounted with ½-inch thick spacer for uniformity.

Make several of these for your outdoor entertaining

LOUNGE CHAIRS

By Bill Baker

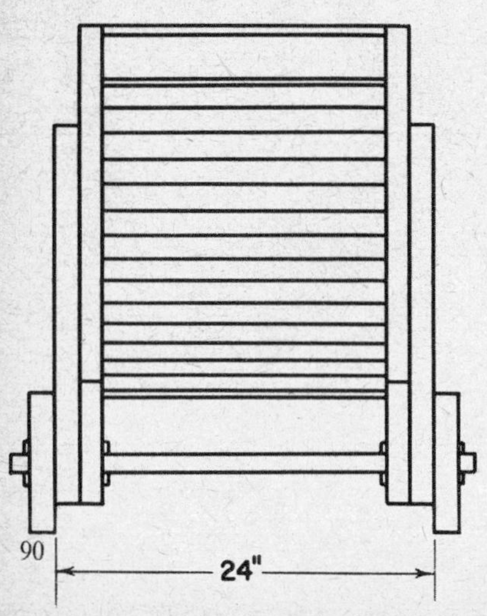

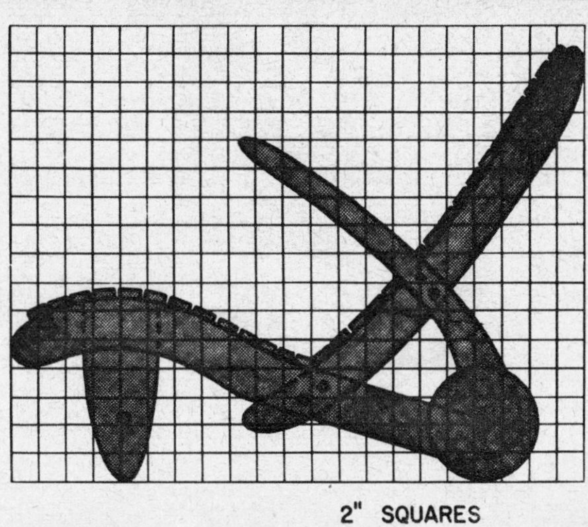

MAKE FULL-SIZE layout on heavy paper according to graph on page 90. Then cut out the various patterns.

PLACE PATTERNS on boards and trace. Also make all holes for bolts, etc. Cut out pieces, mark accordingly.

GLUE BASE and arm with waterproof weldwood glue. Coil spring with sharp ends is used for clamping.

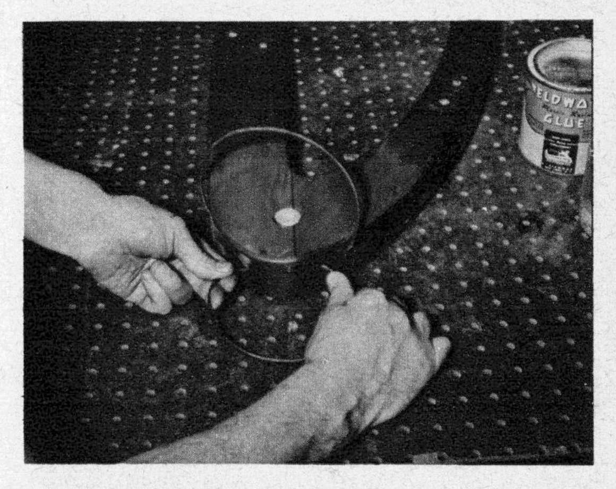

ONCE GLUE is dry and inside of previous assembly planed flush, reinforcing block is then put in place.

OUTSIDE AREA where block is mounted, is sanded on disc sander. Round edges, continue 1-inch hole through sides.

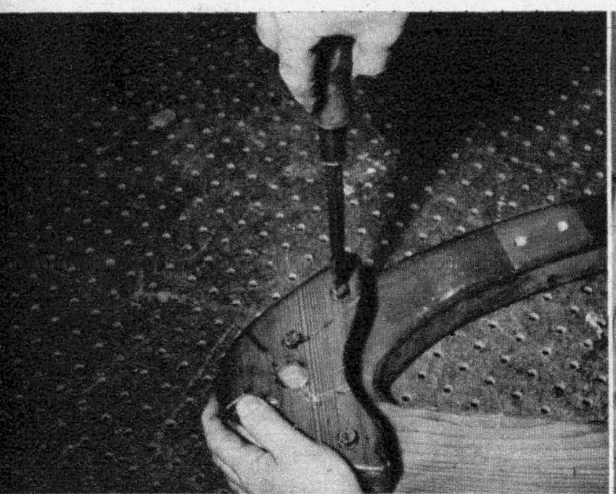

AFTER FRONT LEGS are made, top shoulders are rounded with rasp to contour of bottom edge of seat.

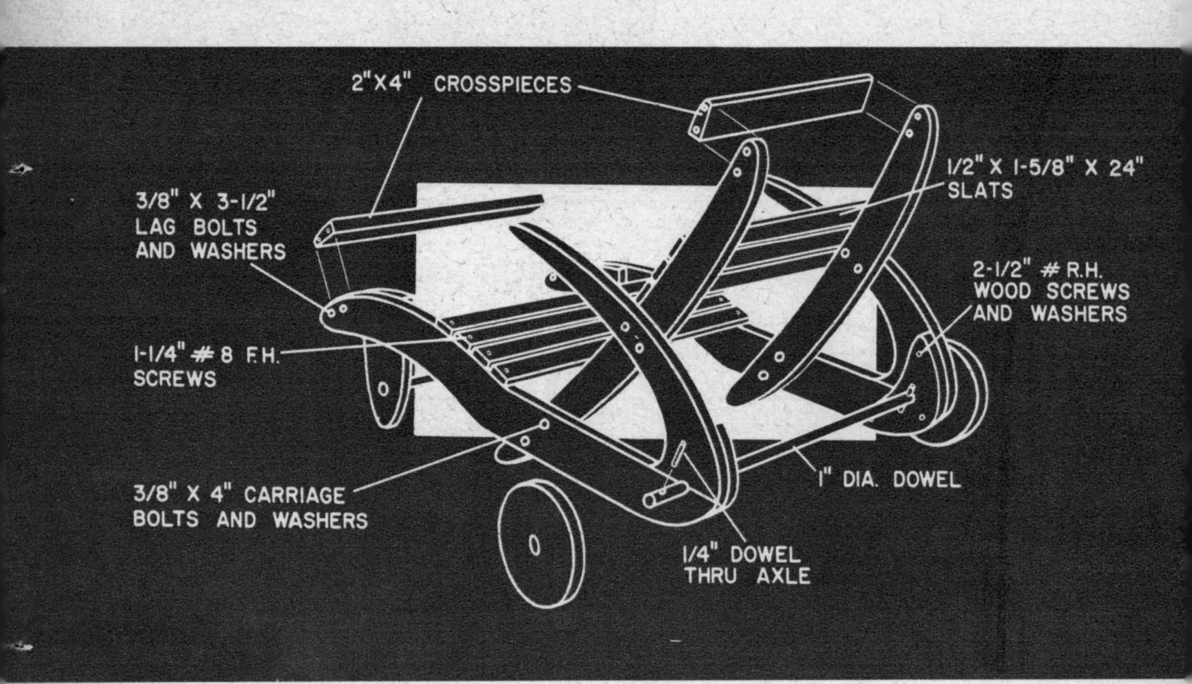

MOUNT LEG to inside of the chair seat, using glue only on one leg. Also use two-inch No. 14 screws.

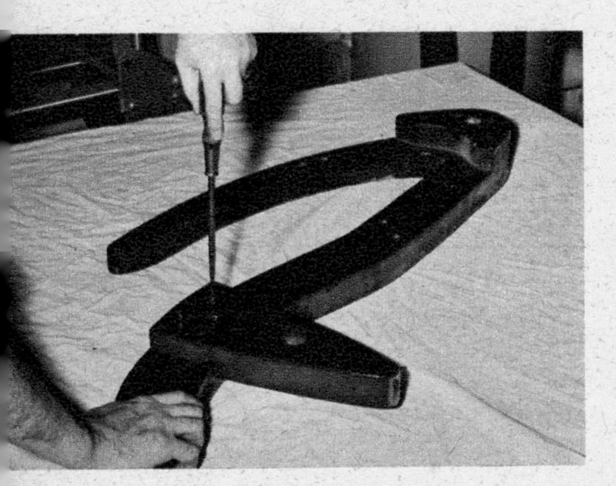

FRONT CROSS PIECE is mounted between two sides with ⅜x3½-inch leg bolts, weldwood glue.

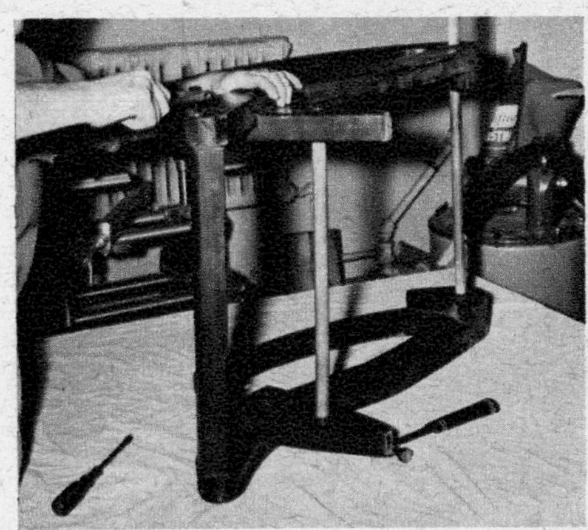

AFTER TOP cross piece is mounted between the two chair sides, plane excess off cross piece, then sand.

CHAIR BACK is mounted between sides which are aligned with a guide strip temporarily tacked on.

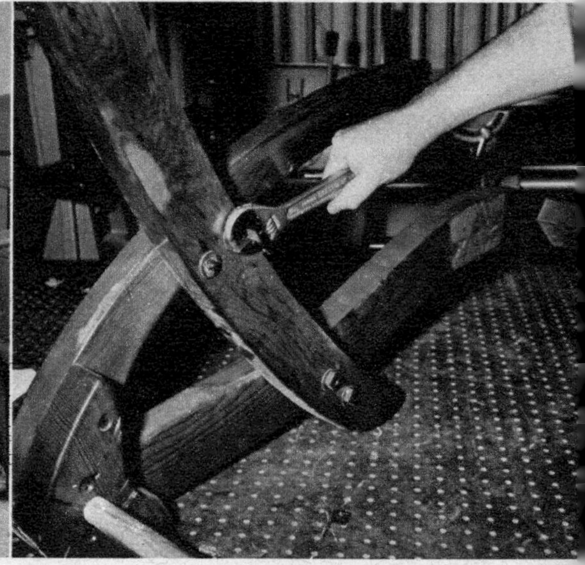

FASTEN chair back to sides with ⅜x4-inch carriage bolts, washers. Then insert 1x30-inch wheel axle.

MOUNT SLATS on seat and back with ½-inch thick spacer. Fit slats on top, then bottom, then between.

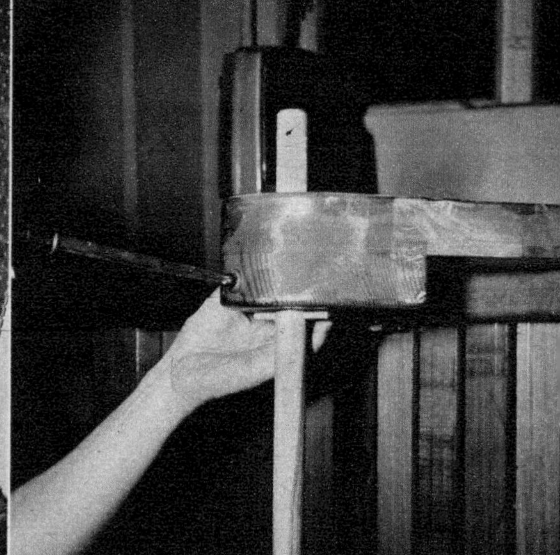

WHEEL AXLE is secured with roundhead screw through block; axle extends equally on each end.

SECOND LEG is mounted with dowel axle inserted in place. Use glue, 2-inch No. 14 roundhead screws.

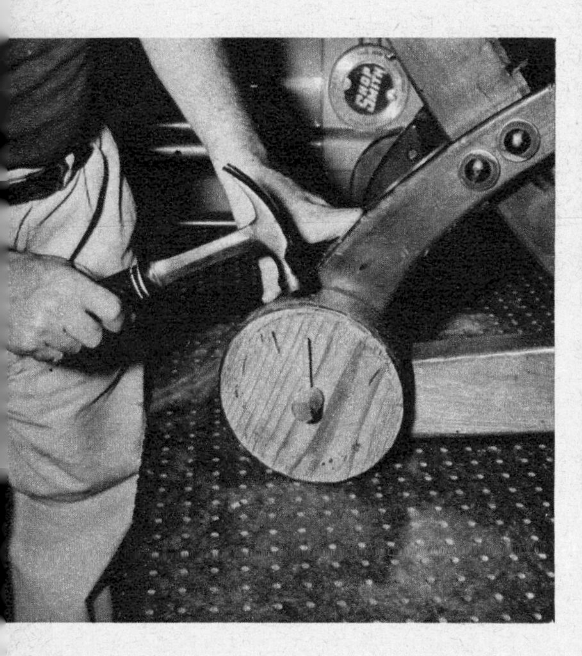

MOUNT wheel stop dowel (¼x2 inches) through axle; keep ⅛-inch clearance between wheel, leg.

MATERIALS NEEDED:

1 board of solid wood 2 inch x 8 inch x 8 feet
1 board of solid wood 2 inch x 6 inch x 10 feet
1 board of solid wood 2 inch x 6 inch x 4 feet
1 board of solid wood 2 inch x 8 inch x 6 feet
1 board of solid wood 2 inch x 4 inch x 4 feet
2 1-inch diameter hardwood dowels—each 3 feet long
1 ¼-inch diameter hardwood dowel—12 inches long
8 carriage bolts—⅜ x 4 inch with washers
8 lag bolts—⅜ x 3½ inch with washers
8 ½-inch washers
8 roundhead screws—2 inch No. 14 with washers
1 dozen roundhead screws—2½ inch No. 14 with washers
6 dozen flathead screws—1¼ inch No. 10
Waterproof weldwood glue; paraffin (to lubricate wheel axle)
No. 1 and No. ½ sandpaper (preferably garnet paper)

Suggestion for Materials to be used:

Redwood, to be painted with special Redwood paint.

Clear Fir, to be painted with Keystone outside enamel

All dimensions of materials are gross—the way they usually are ordered over the counter, unless otherwise specified.

Full size templates are available for this project. They may be had by sending $1.00 to Bill Baker, Fawcett Publications, P. O. Box 331, GPO, New York 1, New York

LAZY SUSAN TABLE

This revolving energy-saver is made of weather-proof Duraply

By Bill Baker

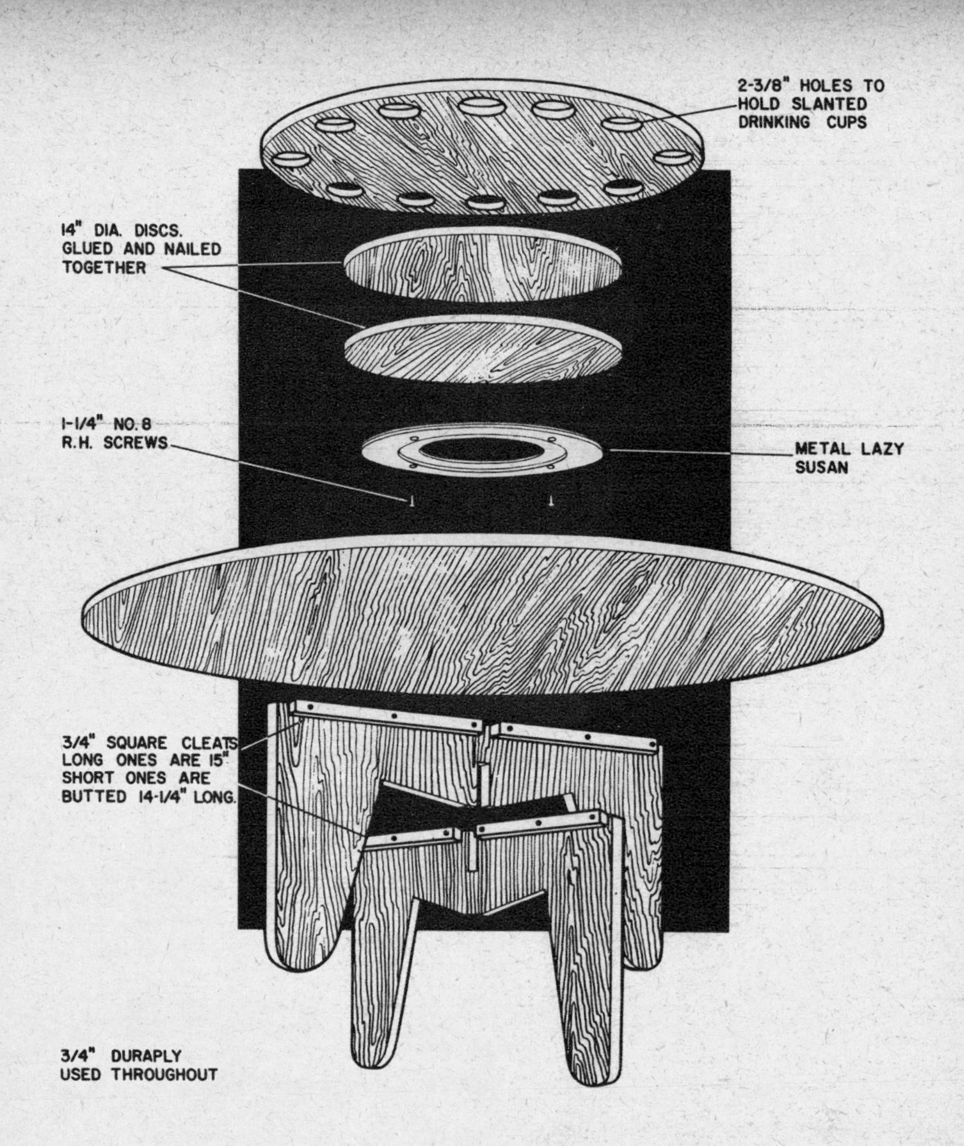

ASIDE from being very necessary for your garden or patio, this lazy susan table will be a conversation piece because it's so original and different. A simple project, it requires a small amount of material and a short amount of time to build. It is made of weather-proof Duraply, thus making it usable both indoors and out. In fact, you can keep it outdoors all the time and the weather will not affect it.

The pattern for the table is drawn full size on heavy paper following the graph layout on page 99. Then the pattern of the leg is cut out and placed on the sheet of Duraply. Next, a circle 19½ inches in radius is drawn on the Duraply. This is done with a tremble-set. Then all the other parts are marked on the sheet of Duraply and cut out. •

MAKE PATTERNS of the various pieces shown on the drawings accompanying this story. Transfer the patterns to a sheet of Duraply, as shown at left.

WITH ALL PARTS cut out from the sheet of Duraply, temporarily tack the two cross leg pieces together. Join the straight edge and sand all the other edges.

TABLE TOP is a circle 19½ inches in radius, as shown below. Edges of circle are carefully sanded as is the entire table top. Sand table carefully.

ON BOTTOM SURFACE of table top, draw line across center; then draw crossline in exact center. From these, make guide lines for legs and cleats.

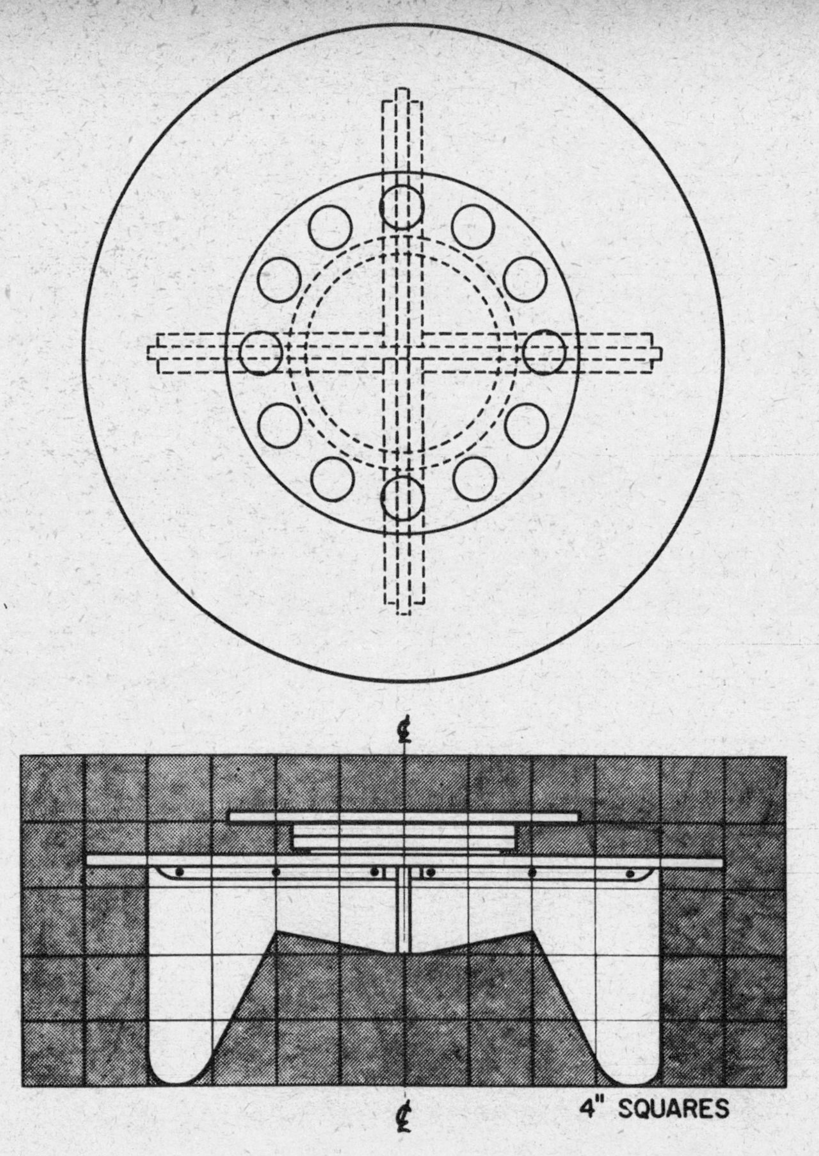

ON BOTTOM SURFACE also mount in exact center a metal lazy susan, available in hardware stores. Buy one 12 inches in diameter, mount carefully.

REMOVE lazy susan bracket from top when you are sure it is positioned correctly. Then round edges of all pieces except the top edges of cross legs.

UPPER TOP has 12 equally-spaced, 2⅜-inch holes to hold slanted drinking cups. Bore holes (with drill press or hand drill) about one inch from edge.

AFTER GLUING and joining two 14-inch diameter Duraply discs to form 1½-inch thick turntable disc, round one edge only. Mount as shown above.

THEN MARK guideline for the lazy susan bracket in center of the turntable disc. Mount bracket to the disc with 1¼-inch No. 8 roundhead screws.

WITH CROSSLEGS tacked together, mark in center, ¾-inch guide lines. Half width should be notched cut on bottom of one leg, half on top of other.

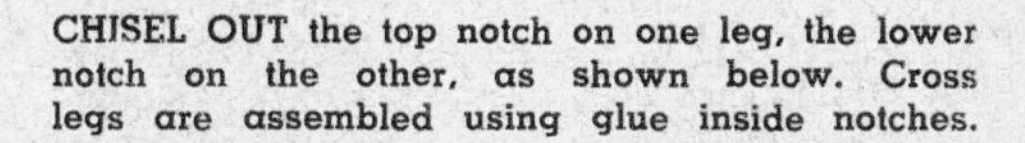

CHISEL OUT the top notch on one leg, the lower notch on the other, as shown below. Cross legs are assembled using glue inside notches.

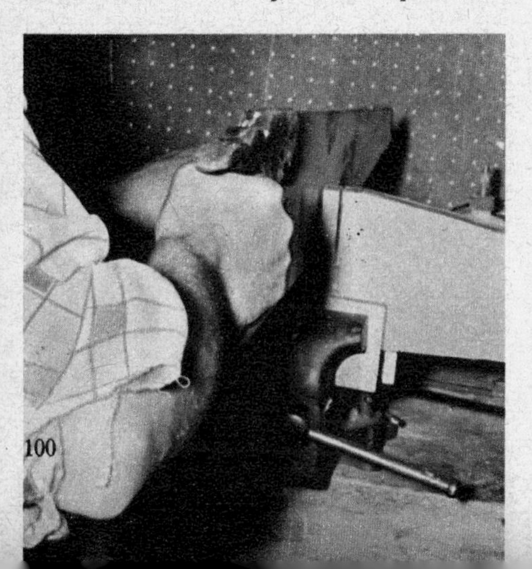

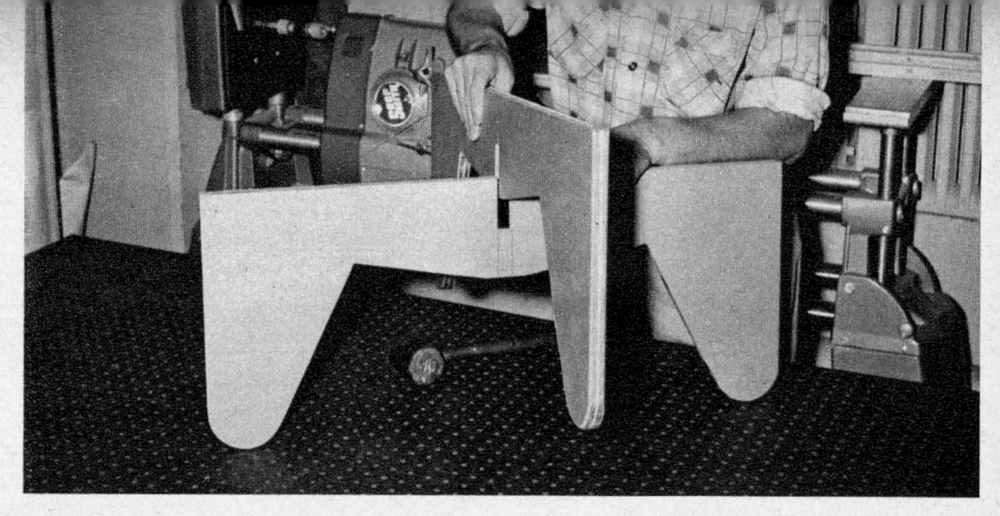

AFTER CUTTING four cleats (¾x¾x15 inches) from solid wood, and four cleats (¾x¾x14¼ inches), round off one end and bore three holes each way and countersink for flathead screws. Mount the longer cleats first, then the shorter cleats; have cleats snug against cross leg and flush with the top edge.

MATERIALS NEEDED:

- ¾ inch x 4 feet x 4 feet Duraply
- 1 piece solid wood—(preferably hardwood) ¾ inch x 6 inches x 3 feet
- 4 dozen 1¼, No. 12 flathead screws
- 1 metal lazy susan, 1 foot in diameter
- 4 1¼x3/16 stove bolts with washers
- 4 1¼x3/16 inch stove bolts with washers
- 4 2 inch, No. 14 flathead screws
- 4 1¼ inch, No. 8 roundhead screws
- Weatherproof weldwood glue
- No. 1, No. ½ sandpaper

MOUNT ENTIRE leg construction to the bottom of the table surface with No. 12 flathead screws. Line up legs first with a guideline on table bottom.

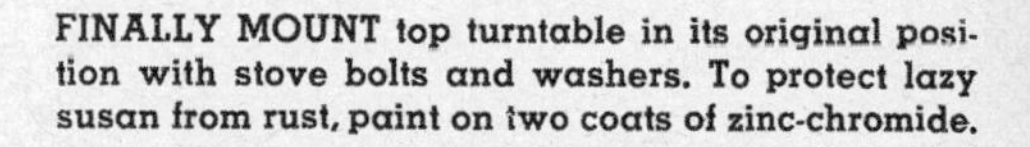

FINALLY MOUNT top turntable in its original position with stove bolts and washers. To protect lazy susan from rust, paint on two coats of zinc-chromide.

LAZY SUSAN UMBRELLA TABLE

It provides pleasant shade and makes for easy serving

By Bill Baker

FOLLOWING the graph shown here, make a full-size layout of one-half of the picnic table on thick paper or cardboard. Next, cut out the leg pattern. Also, set a tremble set or a large set of calipers to the radius of the main top and mark same to one end of one of the two Duraply sheets needed. Next as shown in photos, tape a piece of paper onto the plywood and set the tremble set or calipers to the inside and then the outside radius of the bench and mark same making ¼ of the entire round bench. This will give you the full size pattern for one of the four needed bench sections. Next, lay out onto the remaining Duraply pieces all parts as shown in plywood layout chart and cut them out.

Sand all outside and inside edges smooth, then round same making sure edges are free of slivers.

Temporarily, tack all four legs on top of one another and plane all edges flush. Then place pattern on top, mark guide lines and hole placements. Tack temporarily each set of four pieces together. Again, plane edges flush. Then mark center line. Next place both sets of cross pieces next to one another, hold them together temporarily with clamps, align with center line, and mark the following. Mark a line parallel to center line ⅜ of an inch to each side of same. Next, mark another parallel

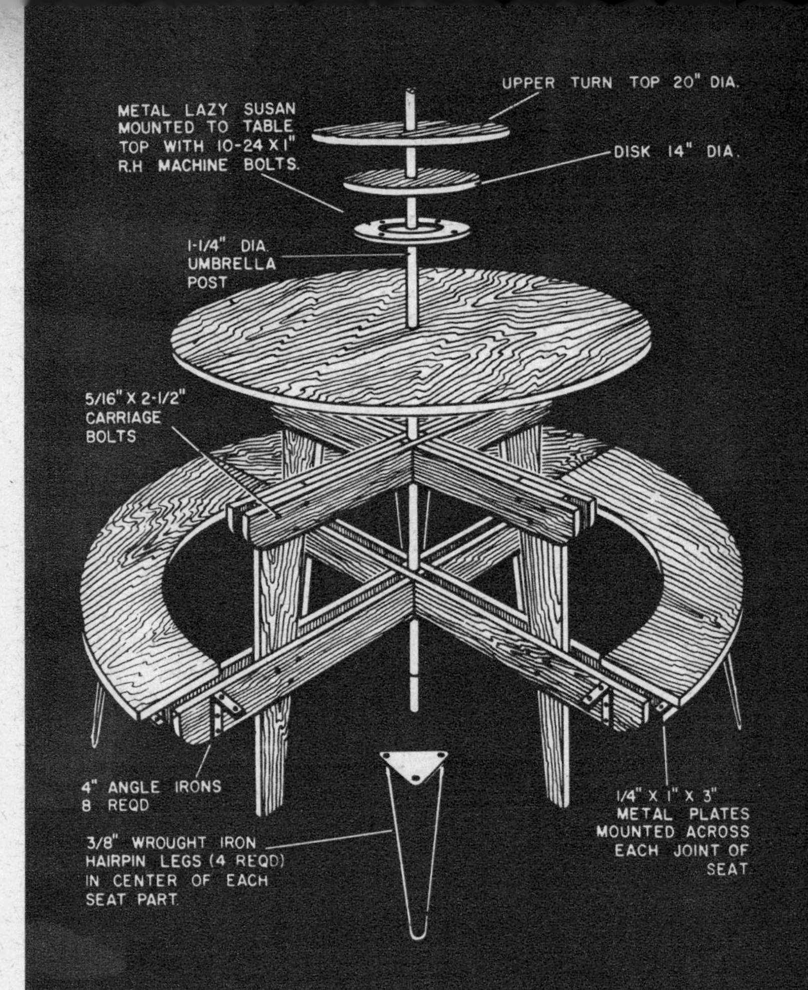

MAKE PATTERN according to diagrams and transfer patterns to two sheets of 4x8-foot Duraply, as shown in photo below.

CUT OUT all parts. Portable bayonet saw (shown here) allows easy cutting of Duraply with minimum effort, moving.

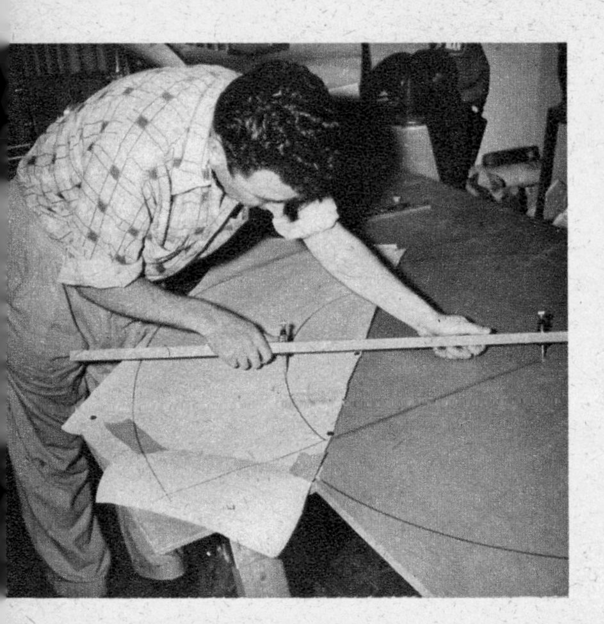

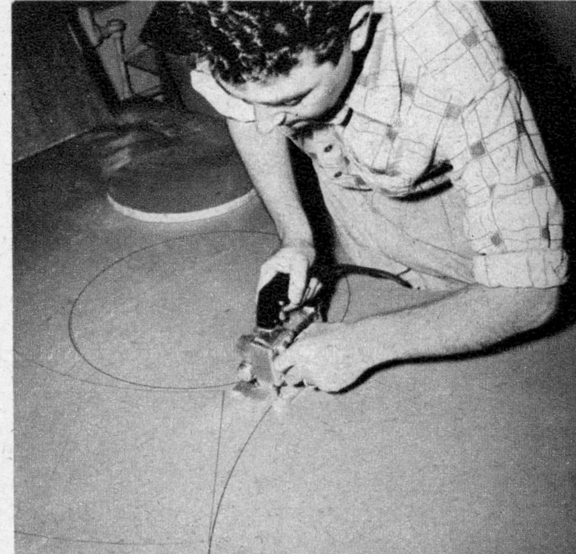

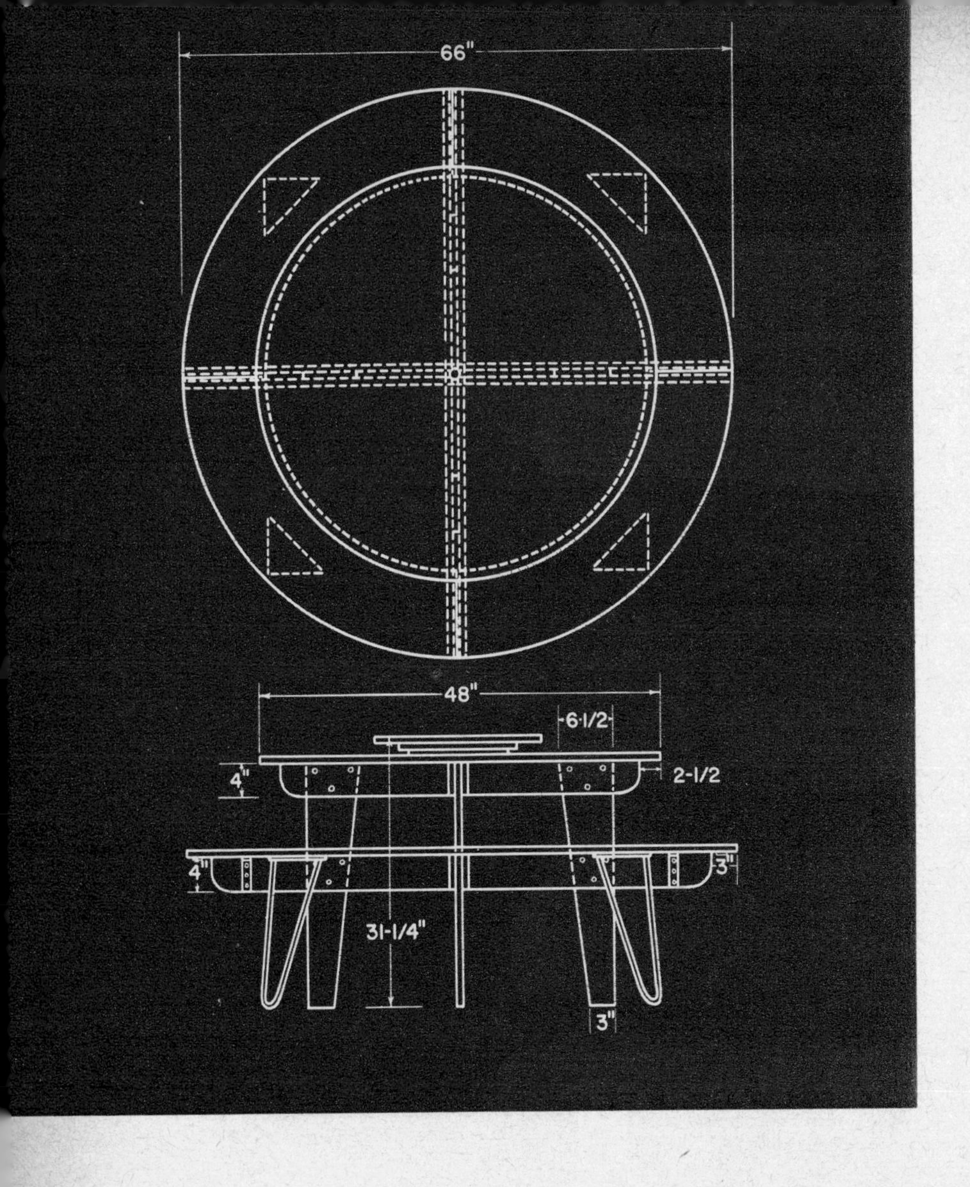

EDGES ARE then sanded smooth. Here outside edge of bench section is sanded on disc sander.

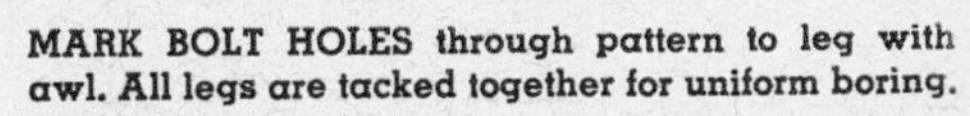
MARK BOLT HOLES through pattern to leg with awl. All legs are tacked together for uniform boring.

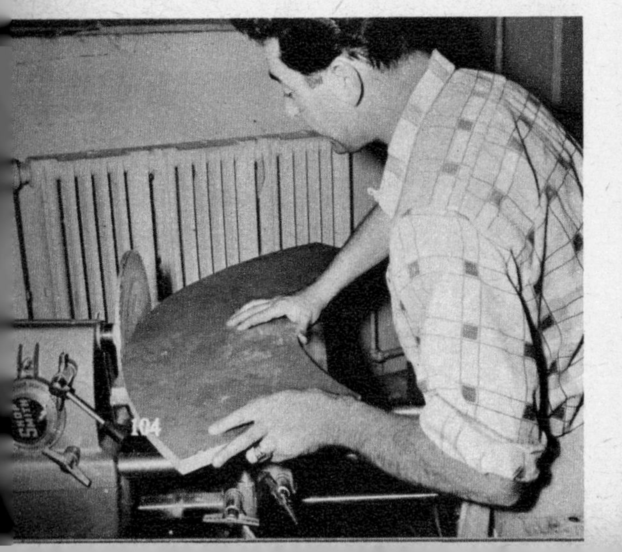

MARK SPACES for cutting of lap joints in the exact center of top and bottom cross pieces, as shown.

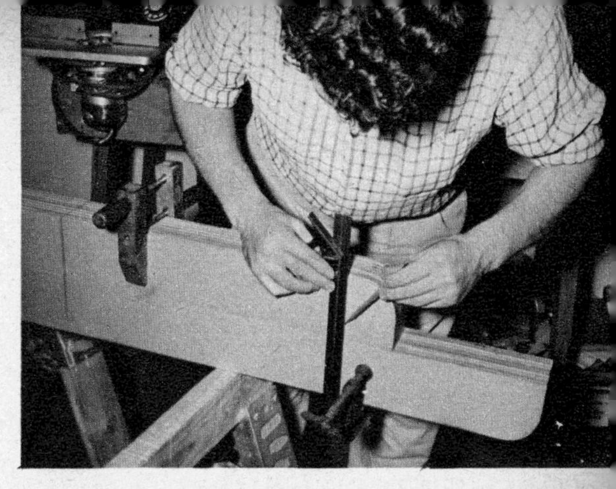

WHILE CROSS PIECES are lined up with center line, ends are marked for location of leg edges.

line ¾ of an inch as shown in photo. While pieces are still together, mark guide lines for leg placement. Place the shorter cross pieces edgewise on the longer cross pieces and mark all leg mounting guide lines to the sides of the cross pieces.

Bore $\frac{5}{16}$-inch holes through all legs. Then take legs apart and align one of the legs first with top cross piece stack. Temporarily tack it on and mark hole position with a $\frac{5}{16}$-inch drill bit through leg. Repeat same with the bottom cross piece stack.

Take each cross piece stack apart and place them together in pairs. Then cut with hand saw, ½ the depth for notches, cutting through bottom on one pair while cutting through top on the other. Next, take all cross pieces apart, and mark the depth in center of width on each side of each cross piece. Then with chisel, notch out one half the thickness from each side to prevent breaking out. Also, continue guide line marks for leg mount on all cross pieces.

Assemble top cross piece first using waterproof weldwood glue and making sure all edges are flush. Next, cover the center hole with a ¾ inch square solid wood strip. Also mount ¾ inch square solid wood cleats between each of the two cross pieces keeping leg mount area free. Use glue and a few finishing nails through the outside of cross pieces. Now, bore three $\frac{3}{16}$-inch holes through each long cleat and one $\frac{3}{16}$-inch hole through each end cleat.

Assemble the bottom or larger cross piece the same way as done previously, but only fill the center hole.

In the center of each of the two cross pieces, bore a hole ⅛ inch larger than the pole used for the umbrella. This should not be larger than 1⅜ of an inch or the pole used should not exceed 1¾ of an inch in diameter.

Mark the machine screw holes of a 12-inch diameter metal Lazy Susan to the

WHERE MARKED previously through pattern, 5/16-inch holes are bored in all four of the legs.

BORE HOLES through top cross pieces, using a leg as pattern. Align leg with guide line, flush with top.

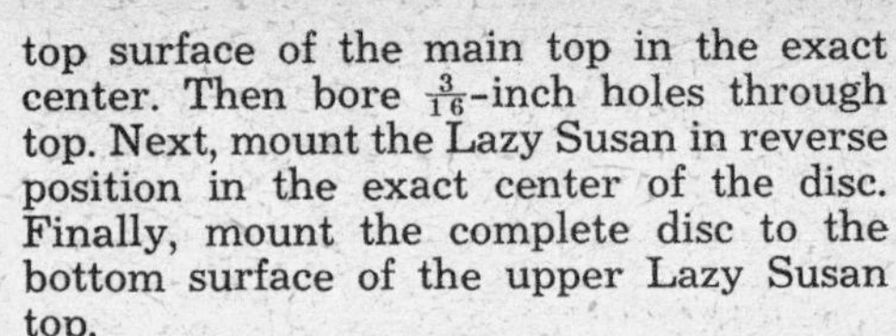

top surface of the main top in the exact center. Then bore $\frac{3}{16}$-inch holes through top. Next, mount the Lazy Susan in reverse position in the exact center of the disc. Finally, mount the complete disc to the bottom surface of the upper Lazy Susan top.

In the center of the main top as well as the Lazy Susan assembly, the same size holes, as bored previously for pole, are bored all the way through.

After marking guide lines to bottom surface of main top, mount top cross piece using waterproof weldwood glue and 1¼ inch No. 10 flathead screws making sure center holes are in alignment.

With table top in upside down position, mount legs with carriage bolts. Next, mount bottom cross piece in position using carriage bolts.

BORE HOLES in bottom cross pieces through leg, making sure that all pieces are in alignment.

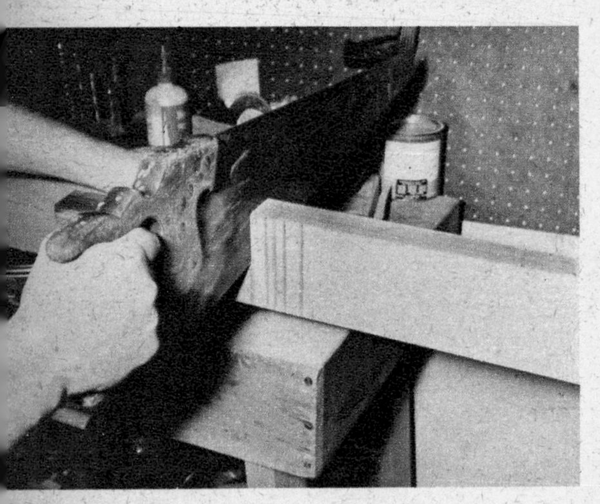

MAKE SAW CUTS in cross pieces for lap joints half way in. Keep cross pieces together for top cut.

NOTCH CROSS PIECES at the exact center of width of the piece where saw cuts were previously made.

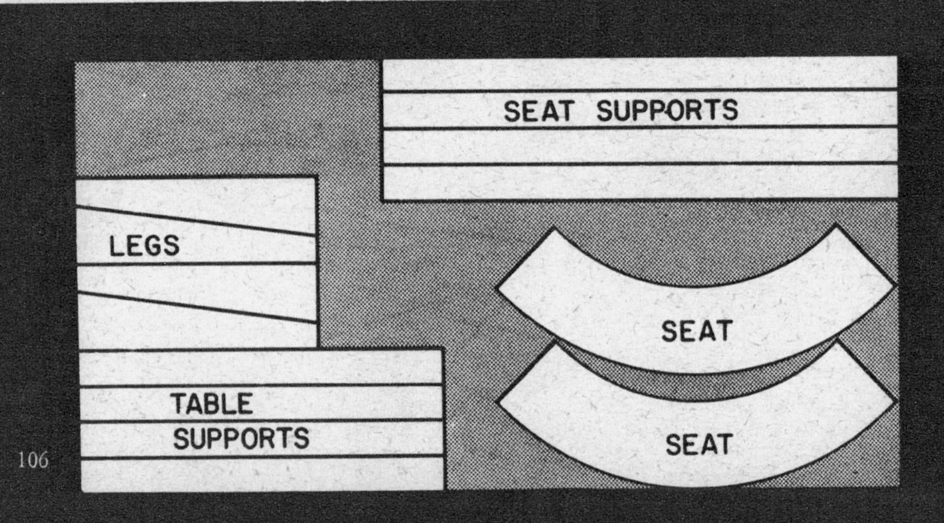

With wood rasp, bevel all edges of leg bottoms. Then turn table right side up and mount Lazy Susan assembly in place using $\frac{3}{16}$ x 1¼-inch machine bolts with washers.

Fit all four seat parts onto bottom cross pieces. Then temporarily tack them in place until all joints are snug and edges even. Now bore pilot holes and fasten seats using 1¼ inch No. 10 flathead screws, countersunk below the surface.

Turn entire table upside down and mount four inch iron angles to each side of cross pieces about one inch in from the inside of the seat edge. Next, mount three inch metal plates on top of each seat joint about one inch in from the outside edge.

In the center of each seat part, mount standard 16-inch high "hairpin" type wrought iron legs. Then finish and paint with outdoor enamel (Keystone). •

ASSEMBLE CROSS PIECES, making sure all edges are flush. Top cross piece is being assembled here.

CLOSE-UP OF cross piece assembly. Since only glue is utilized, make sure notches are precision cut.

GLUE WOOD CLEATS (¾ inch square) between each two cross pieces and flush with the top edges.

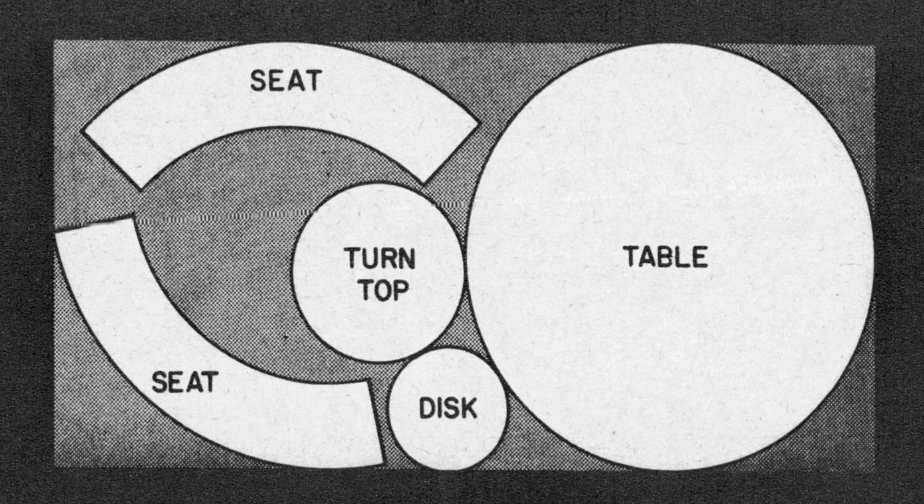

BORE CENTERHOLES in both cross pieces for umbrella pole. Hole size depends on pole thickness.

MARK FOUR bolt holes through metal Lazy Susan to be mounted in center of main table surface.

MOUNT LAZY SUSAN in center of Duraply disc which is placed between table top, upper wood top.

MOUNT DISC with Lazy Susan to center of bottom surface of the upper table top. Use glue, screws.

MATERIALS NEEDED:

- 2 sheets of ¾ inch x 4 feet x 8 feet Duraply
- 1 piece of ¾ inch x 3 inch x 3 feet solid wood
- 2 dozen 5/16 x 2½-inch carriage bolts with washers
- 4 ¼x1x3 inch metal plates
- 8 4-inch iron angles with ¾-inch screws
- 4 16-inch hairpin type—wrought iron legs
- 5 dozen 1¼ inch No. 10 flathead screws
- 1 12-inch metal Lazy Susan with:
  - 4—¾ inch No. 8 roundhead screws
  - 4—3/16 inch x 1¼ inch machine bolts with washers
- Waterproof weldwood glue
- Wood putty
- Sandpaper—No. 1 and No. ½

DRILL HOLE (size bored through cross pieces) through top pieces; make it ⅛ inch larger than pole.

MOUNT TOP cross piece after carefully marking guide lines to bottom of main table top.

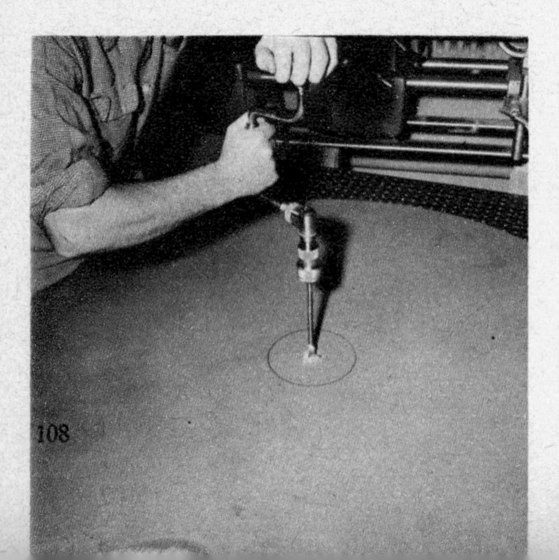

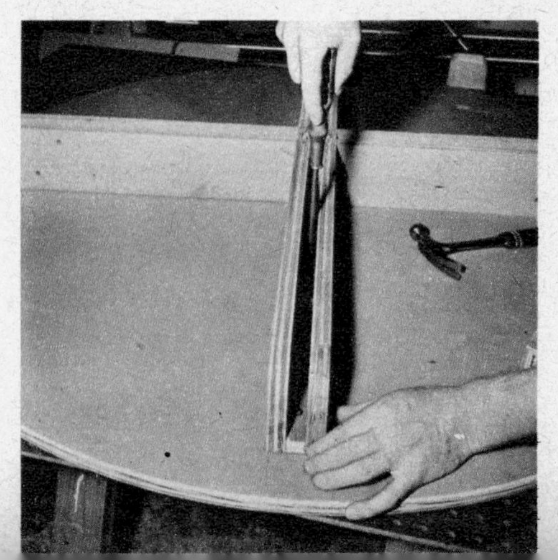

MOUNT TABLE LEGS between top cross pieces, making sure legs are snug against table top.

MOUNT BOTTOM cross pieces to previous assembly. Use 5/16x2½-inch carriage bolts, no glue.

SET TABLE right side up, mount entire Lazy Susan assembly to table top with machine bolts, washers.

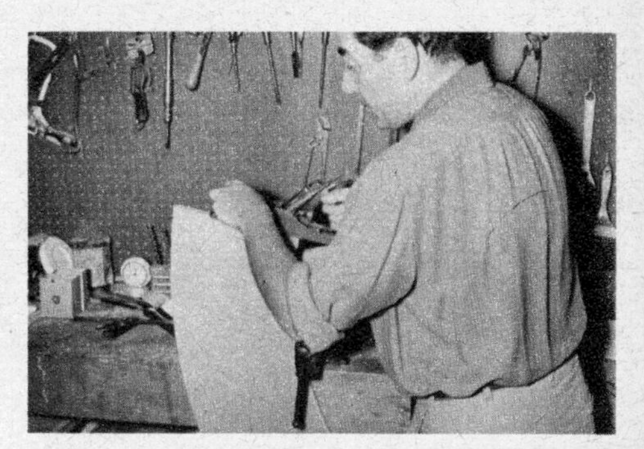

PLANE SEAT EDGES of four seat parts, then fit them together. Use hand plane for good joints.

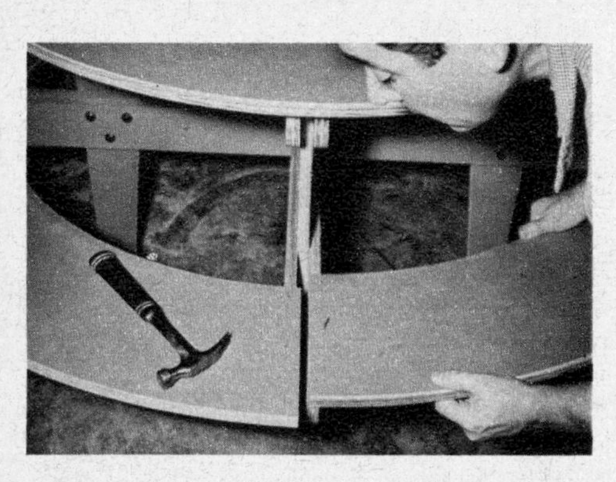

TEMPORARILY TACK seat parts together for proper fit. Align them with guide lines on cross pieces.

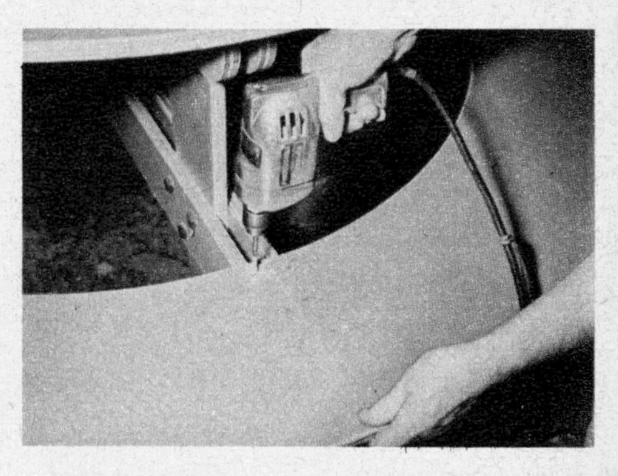

WHEN FITTED, bore four 3/16-inch holes through seats, 3/32-inch pilot holes into cross pieces.

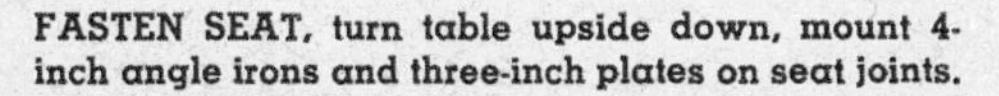

FASTEN SEAT, turn table upside down, mount 4-inch angle irons and three-inch plates on seat joints.

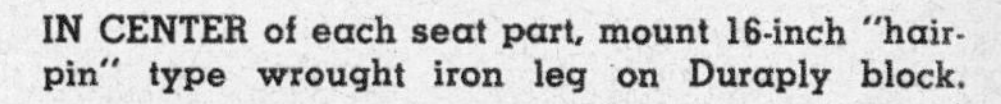

IN CENTER of each seat part, mount 16-inch "hairpin" type wrought iron leg on Duraply block.

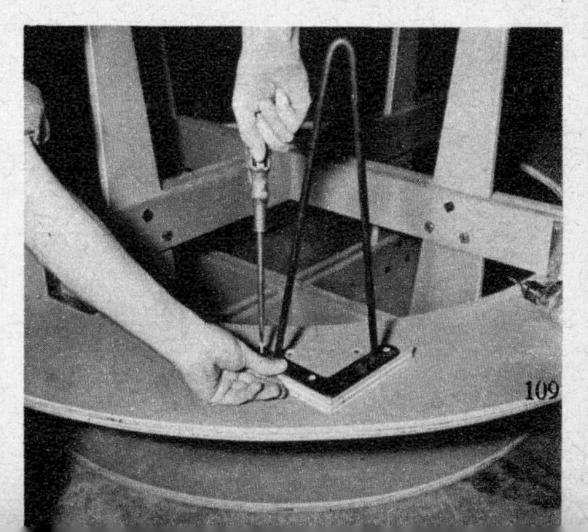

BAR CART

Food and drinks move outdoors easily on this mobile unit

By Bill Baker

MAKE a full-size layout on heavy paper, as shown in graph. Cut out all pieces from Duraply as shown in cutting diagram and mark them accordingly. Next, mark and bore all holes for assembly. Note: Because there are various ways of concealing the screws, it is optional to either bore ½-inch holes, $\frac{5}{16}$ inch deep and $\frac{3}{16}$-inch holes for the use of long grain wood plugs, or just $\frac{3}{16}$-inch holes all the way through and countersunk for the screw head only.

Assemble the top shelf with the top partition first. Then, assemble the back with the bottom next. Finally, assemble both pre-assemblies as shown in photos. For the entire assembly use waterproof weldwood glue and 1¼-inch No. 8 flathead screws.

As shown in diagram, mark, then bore 2⅜-inch holes for drinking cups in main top, then sand them with drum sander.

In order to give the side and front panels a paneled effect, cut with dado blades ½-inch wide x $\frac{3}{16}$-inch deep grooves, as shown in diagram. Now cut the front pieces and

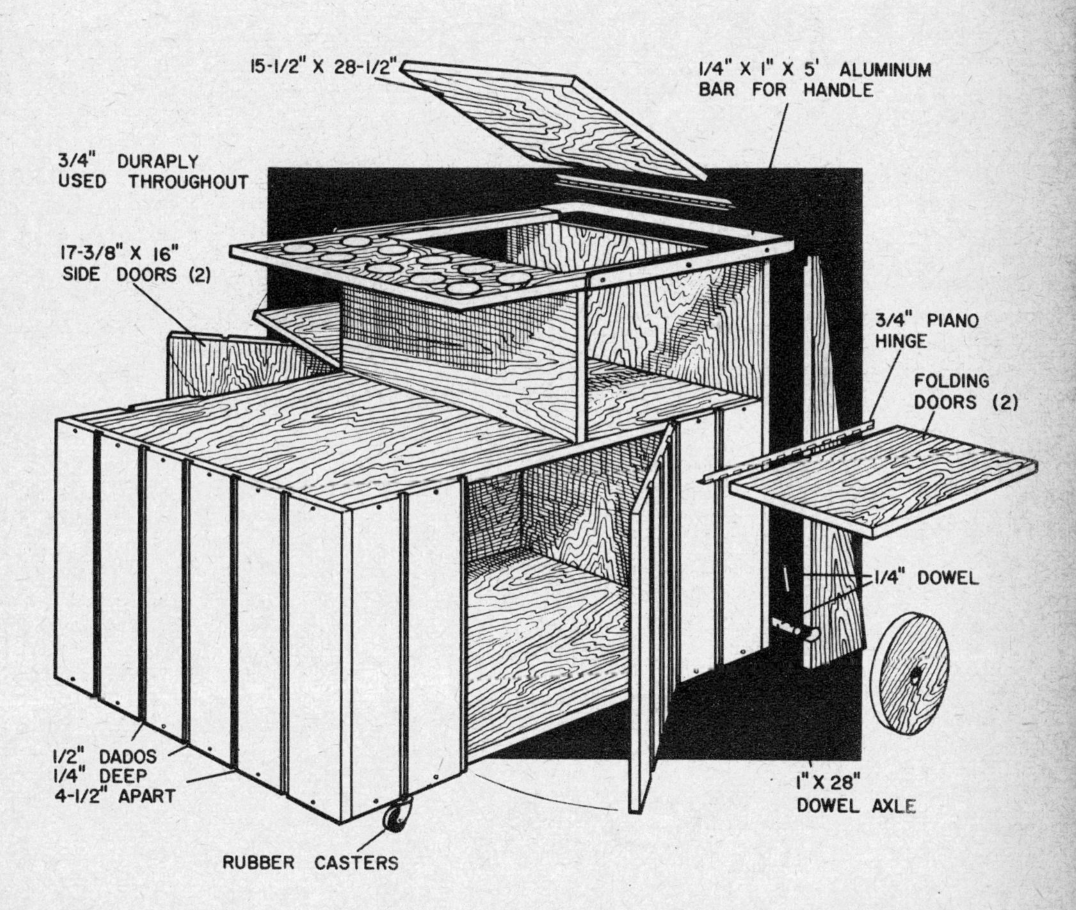

MATERIALS NEEDED:

1 sheet of ¾ inch x 4 feet x 8 feet Duraply (two good sides)

1 piece of ¾ inch x 2 feet x 4 feet Duraply

6 feet of ¾ inch (single dimension) piano hinge with ⅝-inch screws

4 only touch latches

2 only rubber casters (2½ inches overall dimension)

5 dozen flathead screws—1¼ inch No. 8

6 flathead screws—1 inch No. 12

2 roundhead screws—1½ inch No. 12

1 metal bar—¼ inch x ¾ inch or 1 inch x 5 feet (aluminum or brass)

Waterproof weldwood glue

Wood putty

No. ½ sandpaper

All dimensions in material list are gross, the way they usually are ordered over the counter, unless otherwise specified.

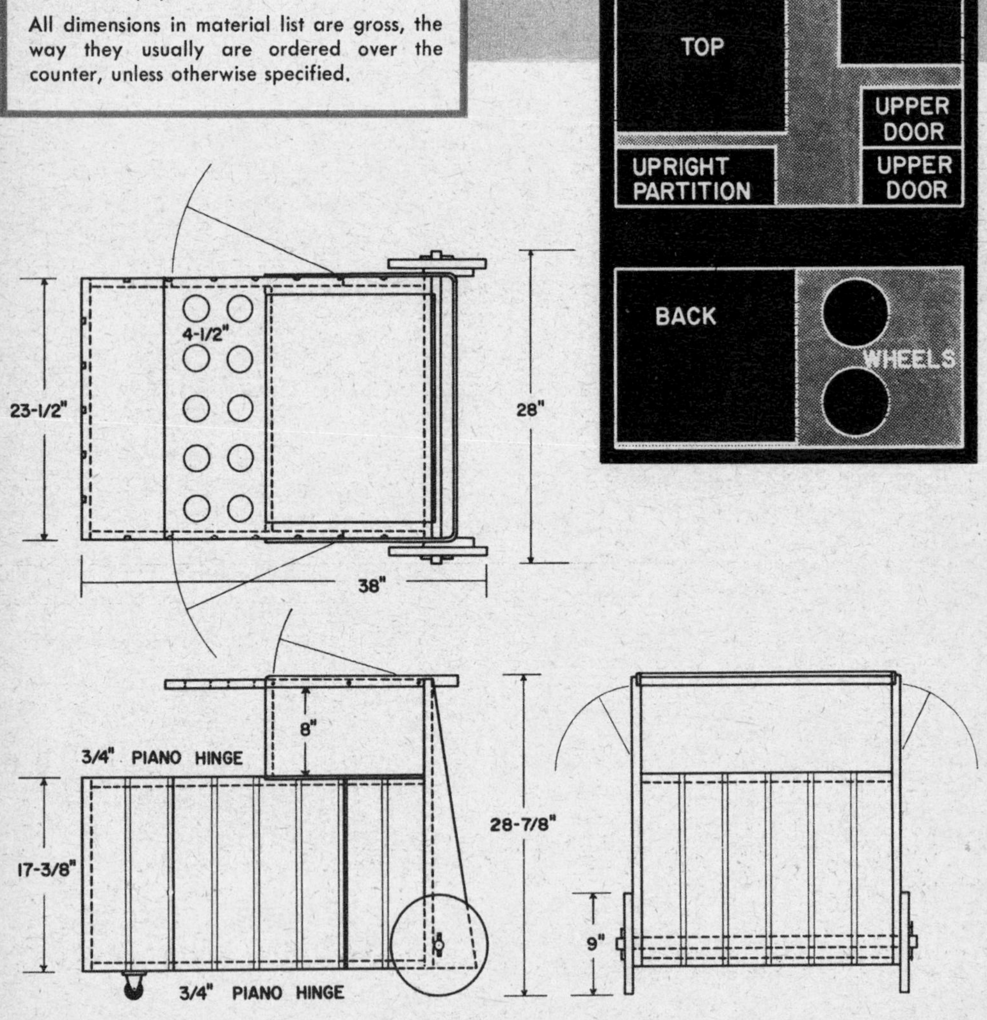

CART BACK is mounted to cart bottom, with parts flush on bottom. Use glue, 1¼-inch No. 8 screws.

BACK ASSEMBLY is mounted to top shelf holding side edges flush. Use glue, 1¼-inch No. 8 screws.

back pieces of each side panel, leaving the door in the center. Hinge the door to the back panel just sliced off, using a ¾-inch (single dimension) piano hinge, making sure that the inside surface is parallel. Note: Before mounting door, take off the thickness of the piano hinge off the back panel.

As shown in photos, mount the back panels to each side of the cabinets, keeping them flush on top and snug against back. Use glue and screws. Temporarily, tack the door down with a finishing nail, in order to keep side panel assembly in line. Next, mount the front panels leaving a ⅛-inch clearance between it and the door edge.

Put bar cart on its back, plane front edges flush, and mount front panel using glue and screws keeping it flush on top.

Mount the main top to cart, keeping back edge flush in back and side edges flush with those of the back. Leave equal amount of overlap on each side of partition.

Mount back fins to each side of bar cart, keeping same flush on the bottom and rounded on top. Again use glue and screws.

Hinge the top doors. Then mount a lid support or regular brass chains on each side. Also, mount touch latches following manufacturer's instructions.

Put bar upside down, insert wheel axle (one-inch hardwood dowel) leaving equal overlap. Then mount wheels. Bore a ⅜-inch hole through dowel axle, then insert a ⅜x2-inch dowel stop using waterproof weldwood glue, making certain there is a ⅛-inch clearance between it and the wheel. Six inches from inside of fins, bore pilot holes through dowel axle and fasten same with 1½-inch No. 12 roundhead screws against back. Leave a ½-inch overlap beyond dowel stop on dowel axle and cut excess off, rounding sharp edges.

Mount two rubber casters four inches from front and side to bottom.

Place bar cart right side up, putty all holes and sand edges smooth.

Of ¾-inch thick scrap wood, make a bending form the same width as main top, rounding two corners to a 2½-inch radius. Also mark the center of width. Mark the center of length of a five-foot long, ¼-inch thick x ¾-inch or one-inch wide brass or aluminum bar. Next, align center lines, clamp bar to form with a wood strip on top. Then slowly bend the bar around the corners making sure the two ends are parallel. Now, bore three screw holes for No. 12 flathead screws and countersink same. Bore holes in the following places: Starting one inch from the ends, then 6½ inches there from, and again 6½ inches, ⅜ inch from bottom edge of bar.

Mount the handle flush with bottom of cart top and align with the top door using one-inch No. 12 flathead screws. Bore ⅛-inch pilot holes first. Note: If a one-inch wide metal bar is used for handle, the upper end corner should be rounded before mounting. •

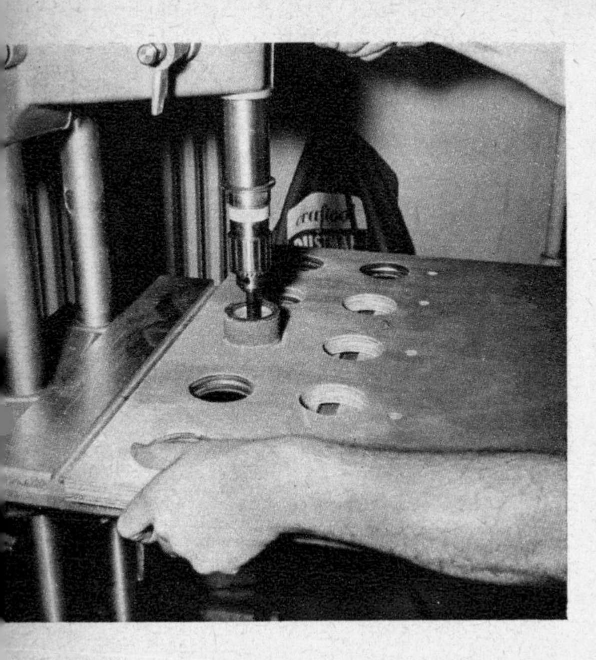

DRUM SANDER is used to sand inside of drinking cup holes in the main top piece. Round off edges.

TO SIMULATE paneled effect on sides and front, ½-inch wide by 3/16-inch deep grooves are cut.

BACK PIECE starting at beginning of second groove is cut off as is front piece at end of second groove.

BACK PART is hinged to door with ¾-inch piano hinge. Insides are flush when parts are parallel.

BACK PART is mounted to cart with door hinged on holding edges flush with surface of top shelf.

FRONT PANEL is mounted in place flush with top and front edges. Leave clearance for door to open.

AFTER PLANING front edges flush, mount front panel. Use weldwood glue, 1¼-inch No. 8 screws.

CART TOP is mounted flush with surface and edges of back, leaving equal overlaps on partition sides.

BACK FIN is mounted to side edges of back, flush on the bottom and inside surface of the back.

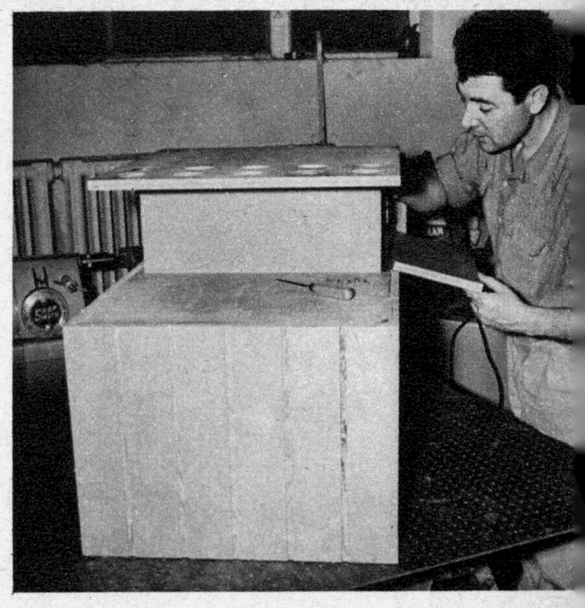

TOP DOOR LID is hinged to each side of cart. Leave ⅛-inch clearance in back, but front edge flush.

LID SUPPORTS are mounted so lids are level when opened. Small link brass chains also can be used.

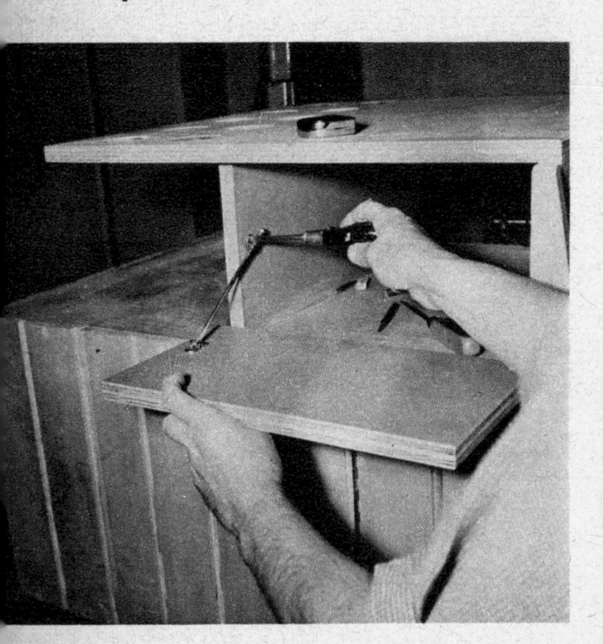

TOUCH LATCHES are mounted on insides of doors and lids so doors can be opened without handles.

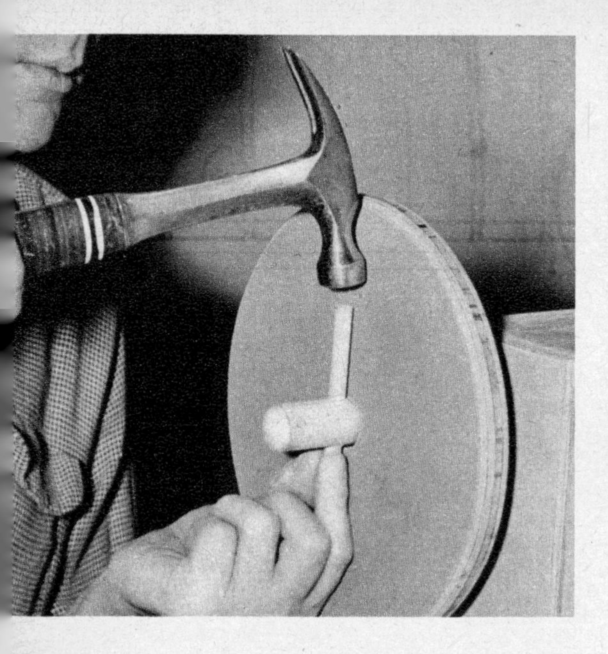

AFTER WHEELS are mounted, dowel stops are inserted in axle with ⅛-inch clearance for turning.

WHEEL AXLE is fastened to cart back with two 1½-inch No. 10 screws, six inches inside each fin.

FORM IS MADE to bend cart handle into shape. The two corners are rounded to a 2½-inch radius.

HANDLE IS ¼- x ¾-inch x 5-foot aluminum or brass bar, mounted flush with bottom of cart top.

PLANTER BOXES

They'll enhance the appearance of any garden

By Bill Baker

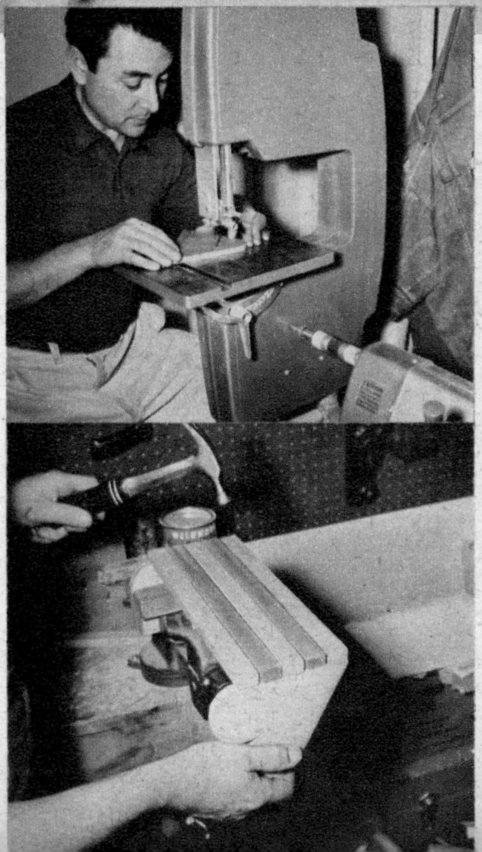

TO make planter box, cut the two ends as shown in graph. Use Redwood or Duraply. Next, cut 10 Redwood strips ½ inch x 1 inch x 1 foot.

Mount five strips to each side of the ends starting at the tip of the heart shaped end pieces and leaving about ⅛-inch clearance between strips for drainage. Use waterproof weldwood glue and finishing nails.

Break all sharp edges. Now mount on the top of each end a pair of small eye screws, screwing same in tightly. Due to the constant exposure to water, it is advisable to finish the planter box with an outdoor paint or Redwood finish. To hang same, use rust-proof wire. •

LAY OUT end pieces according to graph. Cut out on jig saw or band saw, make pieces identical.

MOUNT ½x1-inch wood strips with the outside of both end pieces. Use glue and 3-D finishing nails.

or terrace

STRIPS should be kept about ⅛ inch apart to allow for proper draining of water and air for plants.

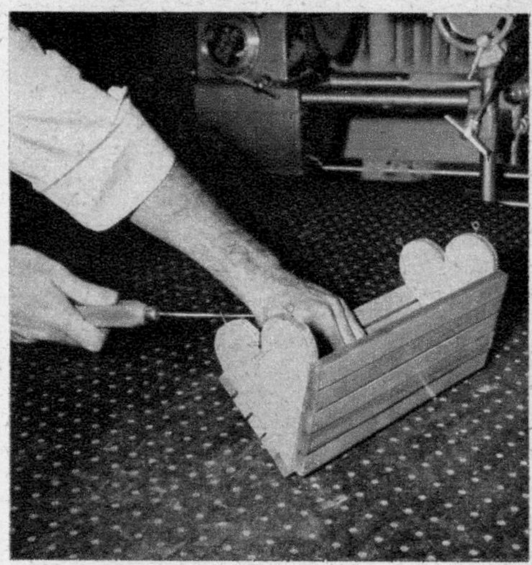

AT HIGH POINT of each end fasten two small eye screws to hold wire from which the box will hang.

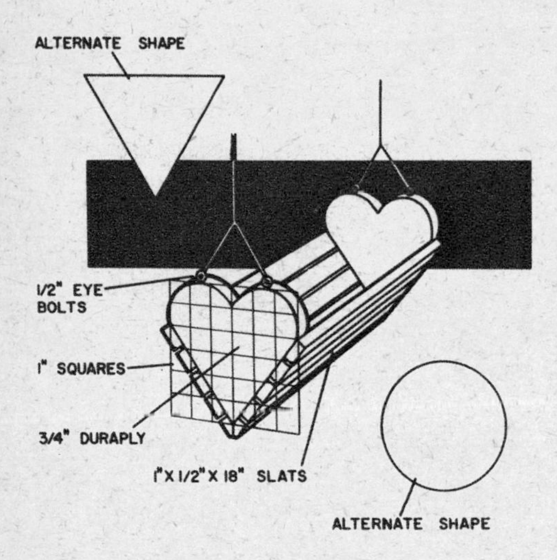

BEVEL all ends with a file to prevent splintering of wood. Sand and round all edges for neat finish.

BARBECUE BUYING GUIDE

A look at the newest products for outdoor living

By Griffith Borgeson

DELUXE example of the trend toward self-contained electric outdoor cooking units is a rotisserie for barbecuing, broiling, grilling, roasting, toasting, frying. It has 12 heating ranges, four platter positions and will handle a 20-pound roast. Made by Finders Mfg. Co. $89.95

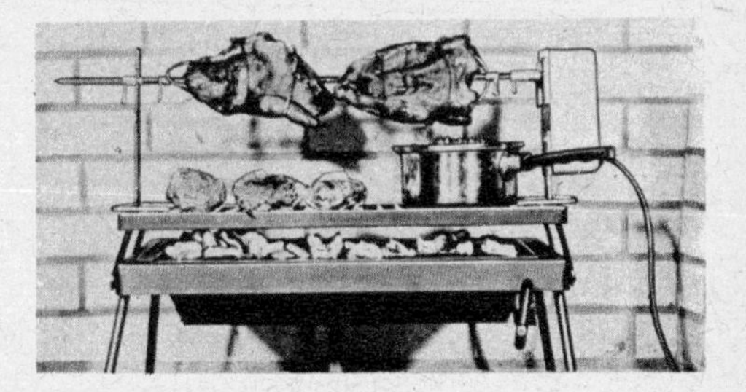

HEAVILY-PLATED steel rotisserie is useful indoors 'or out. The grill, measuring 21 by 14 inches, is easily raised and lowered. Steel legs fold. Maker is Ryder-Elliott, Inc. $34.90

ANOTHER indoor-outdoor economy rotisserie is this flashlight-battery operated model, suitable even for picnicking. By Ryder-Elliott $32.90

COVERED WAGON is year's most sensational outdoor unit. Economy model has four-position grill, chrome-plated electric spit, bake shelf, bun warmer, cutting board. By George Henry $99.50

BARBECOOKERY

IN the whole American domestic scene it's doubtful that there's a more rapidly growing field than the big, broad field of outdoor living. Millions of Americans are learning that the old-fashioned idea of the "back yard" as merely a place to hang the laundry is as outdated as the horseless carriage. They are learning to think in terms of living to the very limit of their lot's boundaries. The outdoor living area can sometimes double a home's useful living space.

An immense industry has risen to satisfy the needs of Americans who have discovered this new living area, with its sunlight, fresh air and green, growing surroundings. At first the equipment was simple, borrowed from beach and camping supplies. Then it became more specialized, more suited to its at-home purpose, more attractive. Now it has reached that stage of everyday acceptance where an area like Southern California can support an annual patio and outdoor living show and even a "barbecue college."

A further trend in outdoor living that has gathered a lot of momentum recently is the blending together of outdoor and indoor living areas. Much of the furniture now designed for outdoor use is just as much at home inside the house; it has reached the "inside" level of style, beauty and quality. Tens of thousands of young homeowners today are furnishing their homes in "in-out" furniture. Part of the reason is purely practical: this kind of furniture will serve equally well in either living area. But just as important is the fact that high-style outdoor furniture often has a light and airy quality that gives interiors a more spacious, less crowded look. It brings some of the space of the outdoors into the home.

One of the most important developments in the outdoor furniture field is the recent swing by the whole manufacturing industry to brilliant colors, gay floral patterns, and super-durable plastic fabrics in bright colors. Even aluminum is now given an "anodized" finish in a variety of colors. These trends mark the final break with the old "awning canvas" era and the real beginning of the blending together of indoor and outdoor living areas in the modern American home.

The same pattern has been followed in the development of the art and enjoyment of outdoor cooking. When the kitchen first moved into the outdoors, it was with the aid of primitive camping equipment. Then came the era of the charcoal brazier. The brazier is here to stay, but the latest new trend has been in the direction of completely self-contained cooking units that can be used conveniently, efficiently and enjoyably indoors or out. And this resulted in the now-booming popularity of the all-purpose electric rotisserie that does everything but wash the dishes. Charcoal cookery has progressed at the same pace, and the "barbecook" never before has had so many conveniences at his or her disposal. •

PATIO KITCHEN of welded steel with baked enamel finish accommodates hand or electric spit, has condiment shelf, hood reflector, two-section grill, Formica slicing boards, adjustable firebox, warming oven. Made by Albert Sales $75

STAINLESS STEEL heat reflector, three large Formica workboards, a big utility shelf are features of this rotisserie-grill. Motor and lamp are extra. Produced by Big Boy Mfg. $119.95

CONVERT-A-GRILL (left) and Convert-A-Fire (above) permit built-in barbecues to be changed from one style to another with no structural modifications. Manufactured by Albert Sales, C-A-Grill is $16.50, C-A-Fire $19.50

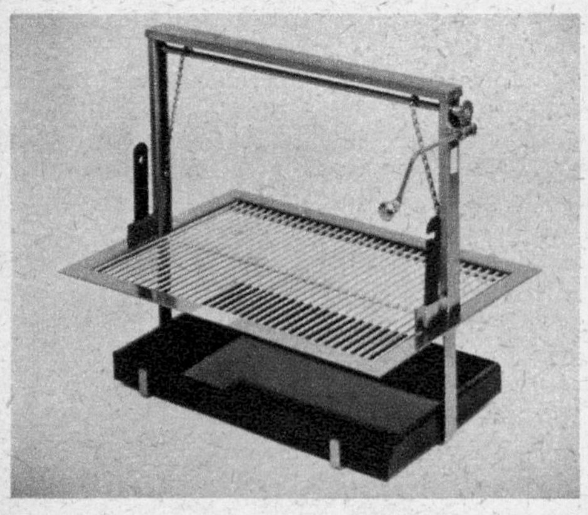

CONTROL-A-FIRE has the additional refinement of adjustability. A crank-screw mechanism, operated from the front, raises and lowers the firebox. Made by Albert, it sells for $22.50. Not shown is Albert's similar Control-A-Grill priced at $19

NEW TWIST in barbecuing is Flip-Grill equipped with a 16½-inch double grill which can be turned with its contents. Made by Big Boy Mfg. $24.95

BARBA-CHARO is an economical indoor-outdoor grill. Grill is adjustable and charcoal pan lifts out. Produced by Ryder-Elliott $19.95

SWING-A-GRILL has a design enabling grill to move in any horizontal plane without affecting the raise-and-lower or "lazy Susan" motion. This gives maximum heat control and makes the brazier bowl easy to load and empty. Made by Albert, low model is $22.50, high one $25.40

TINY BRAZIERETTE, 15 inches in diameter, is useful for outings, fireplace, dinner table. Grill can be rotated. By Albert Sales $6.50

THREE-COMPARTMENT buffet chafing server permits flexible menus, varied assortments of hot foods. It has brass frame, copper covers, water pan, three stainless steel food pans of 2¼-quart capacity, Sterno lamps. By Sterno $129.50

HOTRAY electric food warmer has a shatterproof radiant glass surface that keeps food piping hot for hours and is thermostatically controlled at 200° F. Model shown is 18x9½ inches but bigger sizes are available. By Salton Mfg. $12.95

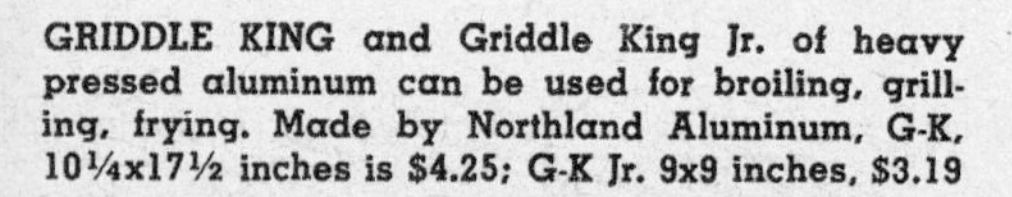

GRIDDLE KING and Griddle King Jr. of heavy pressed aluminum can be used for broiling, grilling, frying. Made by Northland Aluminum, G-K, 10¼x17½ inches is $4.25; G-K Jr. 9x9 inches, $3.19

INDIVIDUAL steak platter of heavy aluminum is fine for both cooking and serving, smoothly-finished and easy to clean. The 8½x12½-inch size fits separate holder, as illustrated. By Northland Aluminum, platter is $2.98, holder $2.49

FOUR-CUP coffee server is kept hot by Sterno container. Stand and fuel holder are polished brass. Comes in 8, 12 cup sizes. By Sterno, $11

HOTABLE is an electric serving cart with one hot, one cool shelf. Top shelf, 24x16 inches, is shatterproof radiant glass thermostatically controlled at 200° F. By Salton Mfg. $49.75

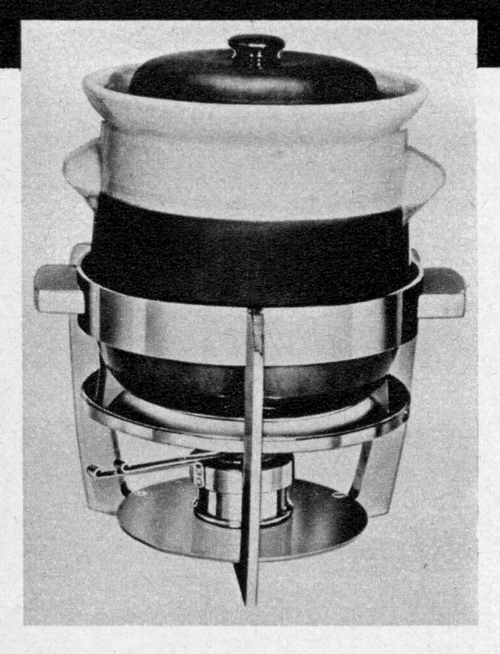

STERNO MARMITE is a two-tone oven-proof crock and cover ideal for soups, beans. It has a six-quart capacity, brass stand and cast brass legs. Model shown by Sterno costs $44.50

THREE-TIER serving cart has electric extension cord, copper-plated steel tubular legs. Height is 30 inches. Produced by Marshmallan $16.95

COPPER chafing dish on cast brass legs holds 4½ pints, has silver-lined water pan and cover. Made by Sterno for $69.50. In chrome $79.50

BIG GRIDDLE (16-inch diameter) of heavy cast aluminum gives even heat for frying steaks, hamburgers, fish. Its handle is stained maple. Manufactured by Northland Aluminum $10.95

SERVING PLATTER of heavy cast aluminum, 19½ by 14 inches, is adapted from a classic old English china platter. It retains all the heat, juices and gravies and can be used for broiling or roasting. Made by Northland Aluminum $12

ECONOMY SERVER has extension cord, chrome steel legs. All edges on top and shelves are double-folded for extra strength. By Marshallan, $16.95

CONVENIENT aluminum stack table has an embossed aluminum top. You'll find it has dozens of uses for outdoor living. Made by Lawnlite......$9.95

TOP SHELF of this 29½-inch high cart lifts out and can be used as a serving tray. Produced by Hamilton, it costs $14.95 in East, $15.95 in West.

TABLE ACCESSORY forms an excellent barbecue work surface with its 18x29-inch Formica top. Fits 22 and 24 inch braziers. By Big Boy $14.95

LUXURY two-tier hostess server has coined aluminum top, convenient rack for bottles and glasses. Frame is aluminum. Manufactured by Deeco..$24.95

SHISHKEBAB skewer-broiler by Beh costs $2.49

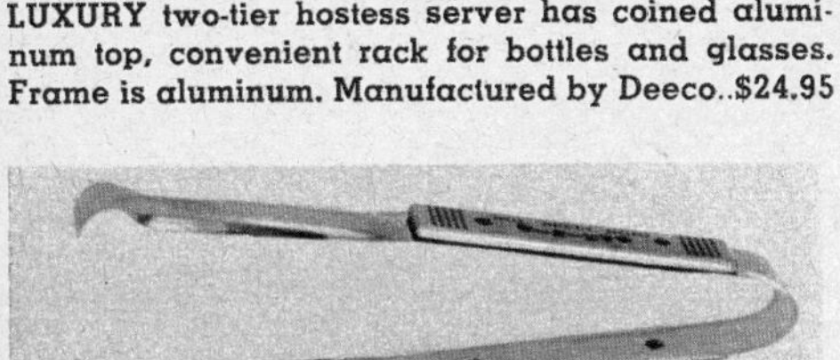

BARBECUE TONGS made by Washburn: $1.75

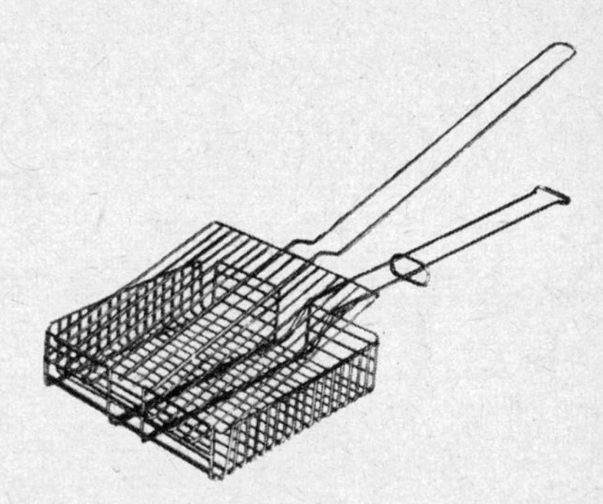

BASKET BROILER made by Washburn is $2.69

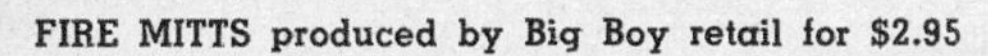

FIRE MITTS produced by Big Boy retail for $2.95

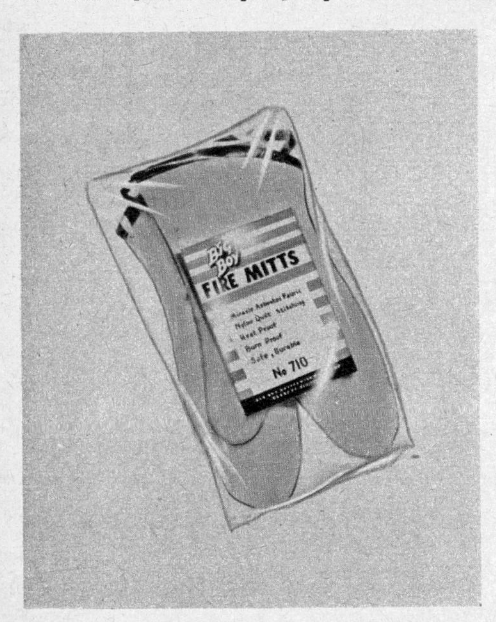

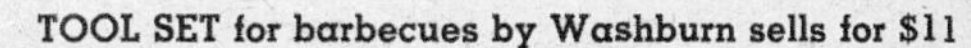

TOOL SET for barbecues by Washburn sells for $11

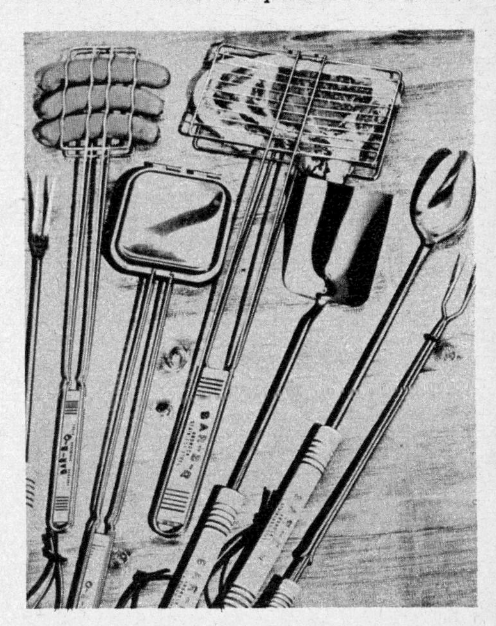

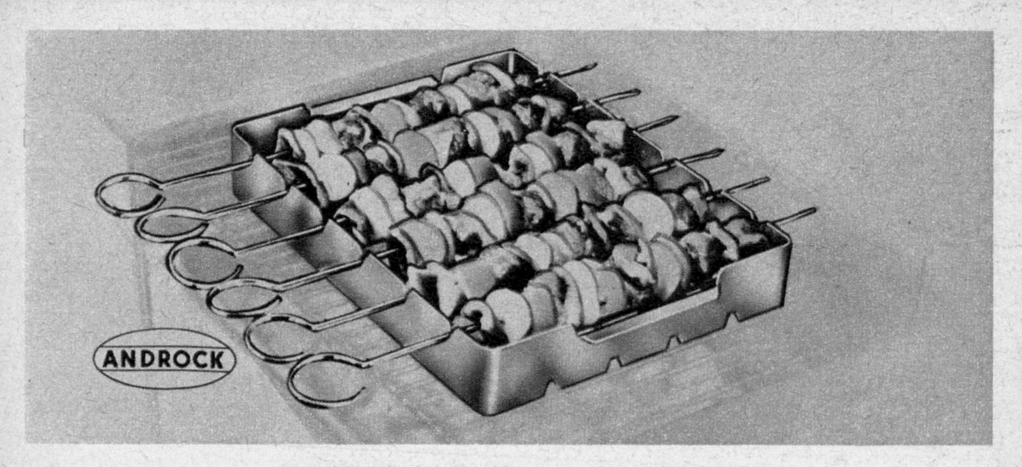

SHISHKEBABER by Washburn costs $7.95

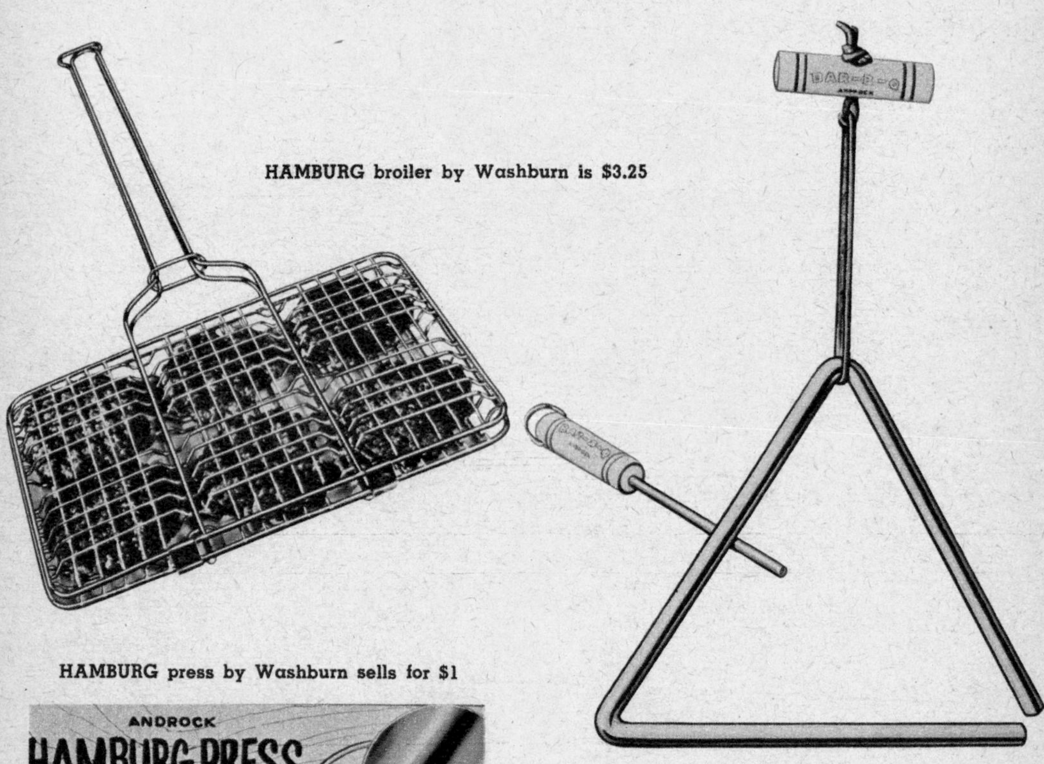

HAMBURG broiler by Washburn is $3.25

HAMBURG press by Washburn sells for $1

BARBECUE gong by Washburn costs $3.98

THE GREAT variety of barbecue accessories now offered by manufacturers makes outdoor cookery more pleasurable than ever. On this page and the one preceding is a representative selection.

NOW as never before, outdoor lighting has become both a science and an art, has received the careful attention of top engineers and stylists. The most dramatic developments have occurred in the field of outdoor electrical lighting, where a huge range of fixtures specifically designed for all-weather use is now available. Many are styled to blend harmoniously with outdoor surroundings. •

TINKER BELL by Kim Lighting sells for $12.95

COPPER Wrenhouse, Kim's 60-watt model, is $21

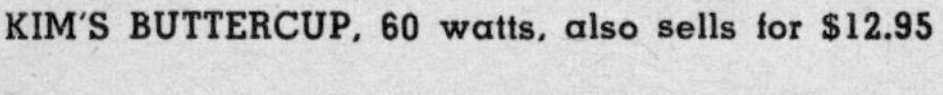

KIM'S BUTTERCUP, 60 watts, also sells for $12.95

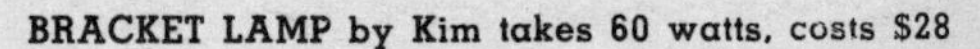

BRACKET LAMP by Kim takes 60 watts, costs $28

BRACKET LANTERN by Kim takes 60 watts, is $34

HALF-SHIELD up-light by Kim, 150 watts, is $21

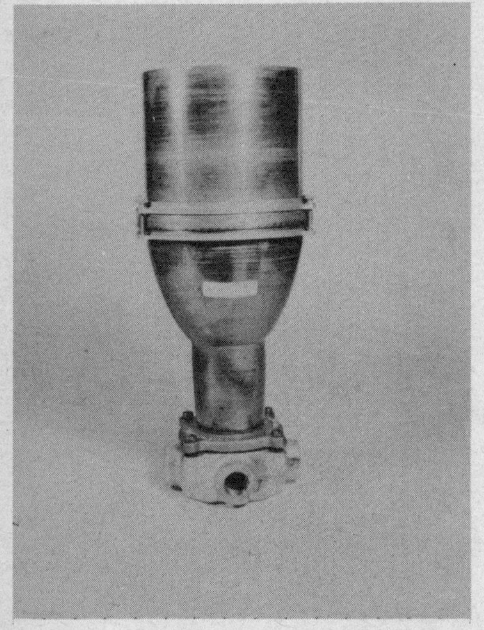

JUNCTION box up-light, also Kim's, sells for $26

TILE up-light by Kim, 150 watts, retails for $38

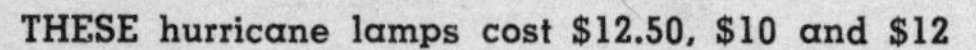

THESE hurricane lamps cost $12.50, $10 and $12

THIS decorative double hurricane stand costs $15

HURRICANE LAMPS long a favorite for outdoor lighting, are extremely convenient because they need no wiring, lend an air of elegance and grace. Those shown above are manufactured by Richard Sandfort.

PRISCILLA Tropic Torch is available in 6 and 7-inch diameters and in copper or aluminum finish. When special fuel is used, torches repel insects. Manufactured by Beh & Co., retails at $4.95-$6.95

HAWAIIAN torches stand 7 feet high, have black matte finish. These are extremely portable and can be used for night picnics and beach parties. They're manufactured by Albert Sales $7.95

GOOD QUALITY chaise ($21.95 including pad) has strong tubular cross-members, sturdy adjustment straps, high-quality back hinges—all of which contribute to rigidity, long life. Each spring band has spring on one end only.

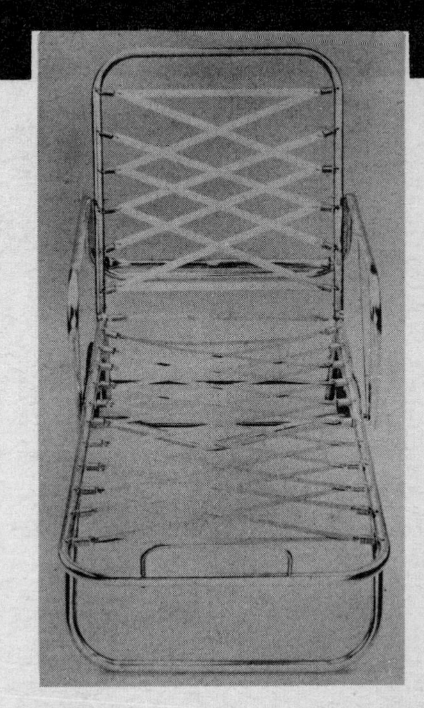

BETTER QUALITY ($24.95 with pad) has same basic structural features and in addition has a spring at end of each band plus extra diagonal bands to distribute loads. Each band can now support a weight of at least 156 pounds before tension will be permanently affected. Note pad bar at front.

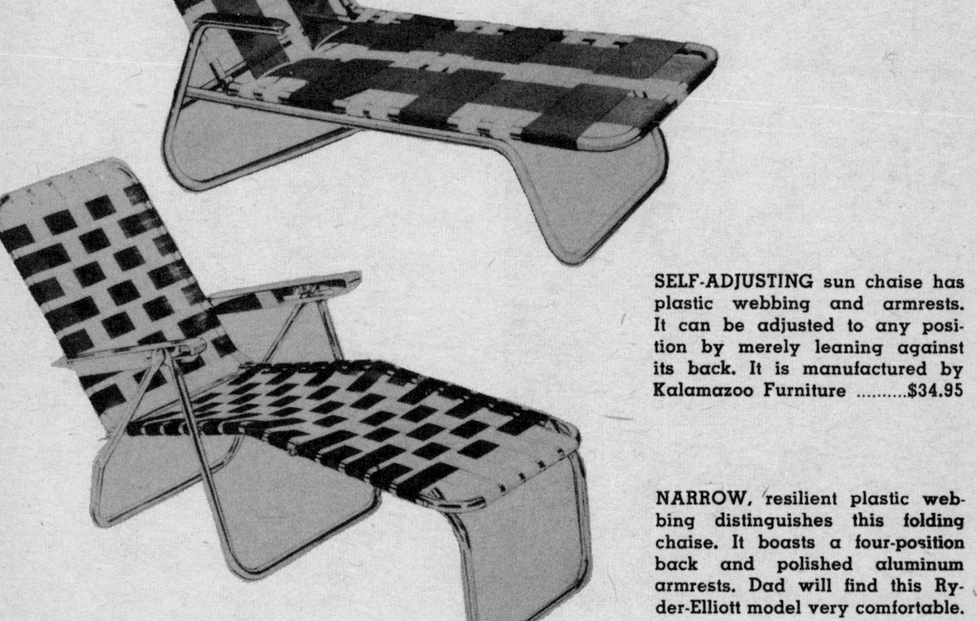

SELF-ADJUSTING sun chaise has plastic webbing and armrests. It can be adjusted to any position by merely leaning against its back. It is manufactured by Kalamazoo Furniture $34.95

NARROW, resilient plastic webbing distinguishes this folding chaise. It boasts a four-position back and polished aluminum armrests. Dad will find this Ryder-Elliott model very comfortable.

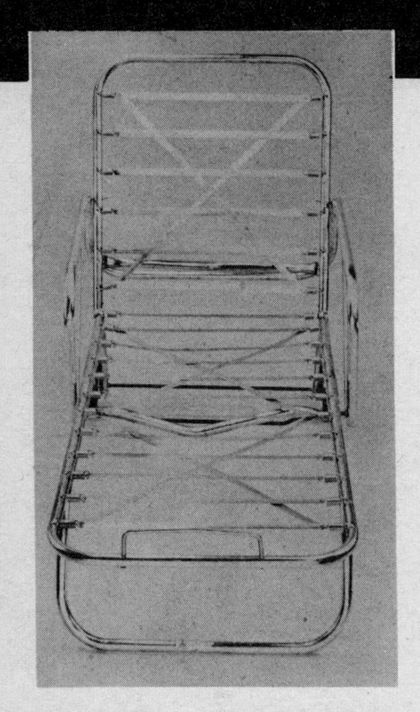

BEST QUALITY ($32.95 with pad) has diagonal bands throughout. Load on any one band is distributed over three springs capable of supporting 234 pounds without losing tension. It's easy to see why this construction is more durable as well as more costly. Any one of the three models, though, is an excellent buy.

RECENTLY huge strides have been made in the design and variety of furniture made from aluminum tubing. Canvas coverings have been replaced almost entirely by brilliantly-hued plastics that are not only more colorful but also more durable. Extruded aluminum shapes have been discovered by many furniture manufacturers and are now in wide use as armrests.

There is more emphasis than ever before on stability. In previous years some chairs made of curved aluminum tubing had a strong tendency to rock, even though they were not intended to be rockers. Now many chairs have sharp right-angle bends in the tubing to eliminate tendency to "tippiness."

Perhaps the most impressive thing about outdoor aluminum furniture today is the great variety of designs and prices that vigorous competition has produced.

In outdoor furniture, as everywhere, price is determined by quality. When you're shopping for furniture made of aluminum tubing, the first thing to note is the strength of the frame. Compare the thickness of the walls of the tubing on a low-priced chair with that of a chair that costs a dollar or two more. You'll probably find that the costlier chair has a "base" made of tubing with almost twice the wall-thickness of the cheaper article. This thickness means greater strength, more years of satisfactory service.

Folding furniture and pieces with adjustable backs should be checked carefully for solid construction. Some folding joints are made simply by running a bolt or rivet through holes in two pieces of tubing, while other joints use cast, machined hardware. You pay more for the second kind, but it pays you back with longer service.

Another area of built-in quality that costs both you and the maker money is banding and springing. At the top of this page and the one opposite are shown three grades of chaise banding and springing. All three chaises are built by one manufacturer, Harlew Manufacturing Co. •

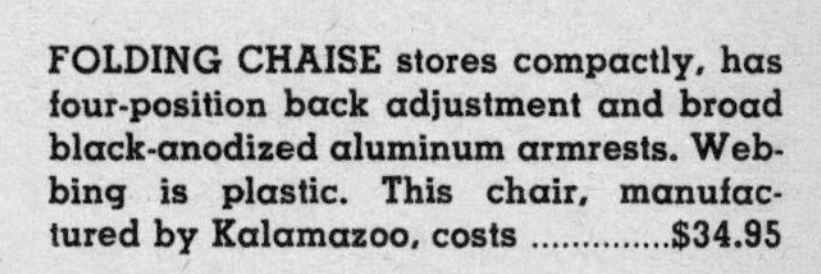

FOLDING CHAISE stores compactly, has four-position back adjustment and broad black-anodized aluminum armrests. Webbing is plastic. This chair, manufactured by Kalamazoo, costs $34.95

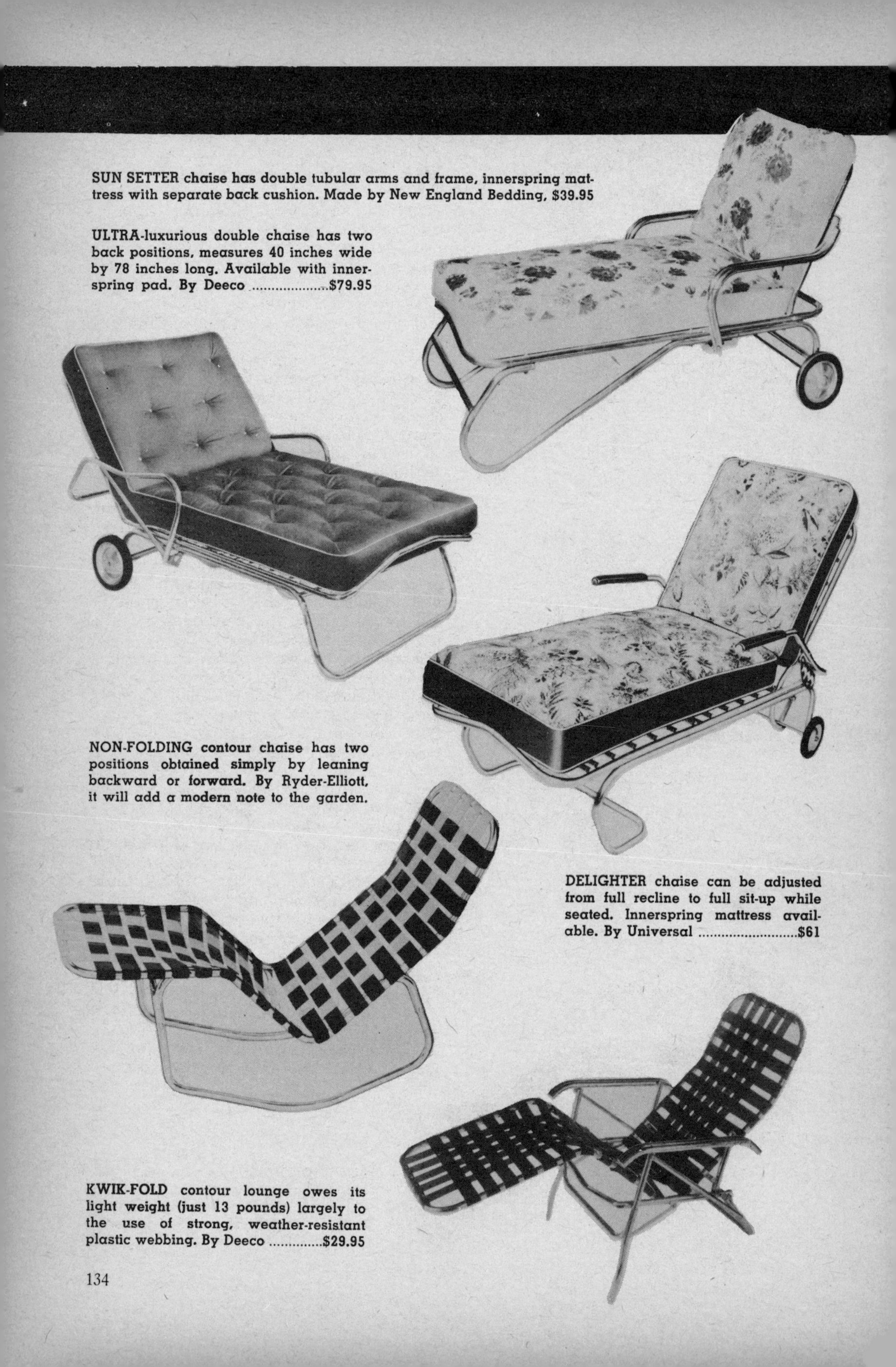

SUN SETTER chaise has double tubular arms and frame, innerspring mattress with separate back cushion. Made by New England Bedding, $39.95

ULTRA-luxurious double chaise has two back positions, measures 40 inches wide by 78 inches long. Available with innerspring pad. By Deeco $79.95

NON-FOLDING contour chaise has two positions obtained simply by leaning backward or forward. By Ryder-Elliott, it will add a modern note to the garden.

DELIGHTER chaise can be adjusted from full recline to full sit-up while seated. Innerspring mattress available. By Universal $61

KWIK-FOLD contour lounge owes its light weight (just 13 pounds) largely to the use of strong, weather-resistant plastic webbing. By Deeco $29.95

THREE-passenger rocker settee is 67½ inches wide with cushions in a wide assortment of fabrics and colors. It is manufactured by Deeco, Inc. $69.95

LIGHTWEIGHT settee tips scales at 27 pounds, seats three in comfort. Circle motif adds a great deal of style and distinction. This model, by Deeco, costs $44.95

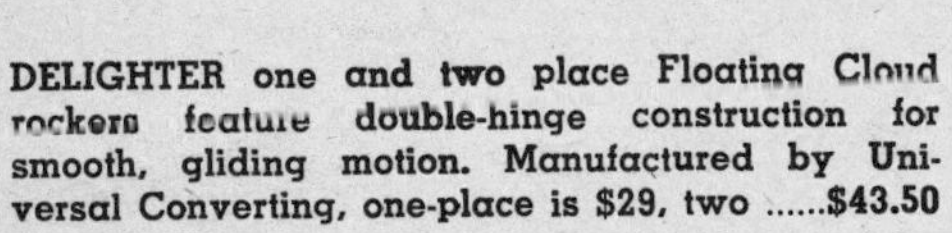

DELIGHTER one and two place Floating Cloud rockers feature double-hinge construction for smooth, gliding motion. Manufactured by Universal Converting, one-place is $29, two $43.50

ONE-PLACE rocker with ball-bearing action is available in choice of box-spring cushions or plastic webbing. By Lawnlite, one with webbing costs $19.95, model with cushions $39.95

ZEPHYR SETTEE is 67½ inches wide and is sold in a choice of innerspring or plain pads. This model is made by Deeco and sells for $59.95

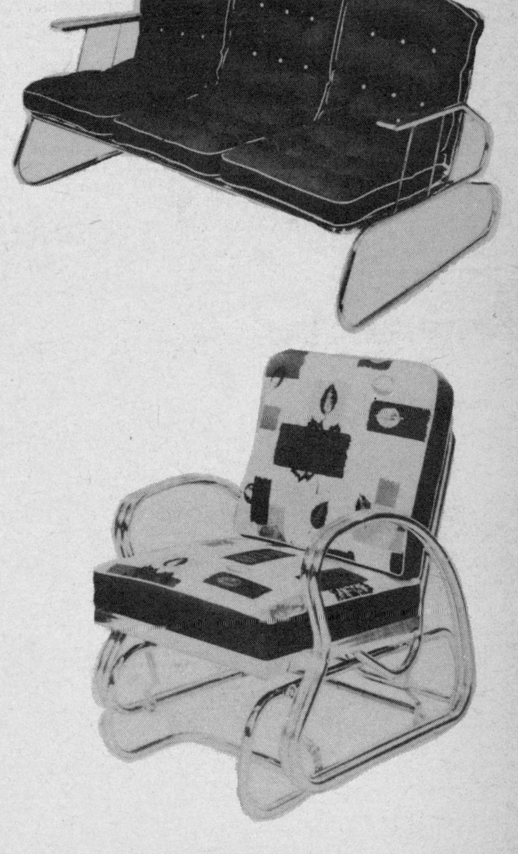

DELUXE director's chair folds with one motion, weighs about seven pounds. The fabric is sailcloth with white piping. Manufactured by Deeco, it costs $14.95

RIGIDLY BRACED one-person rocker weighs approximately 11 pounds. Made by Deeco, its price is $19.95

CIRCLE BARREL chair is a tubular aluminum version of the popular captain's chair design. Deeco manufactures this one also and it is priced at $17.95

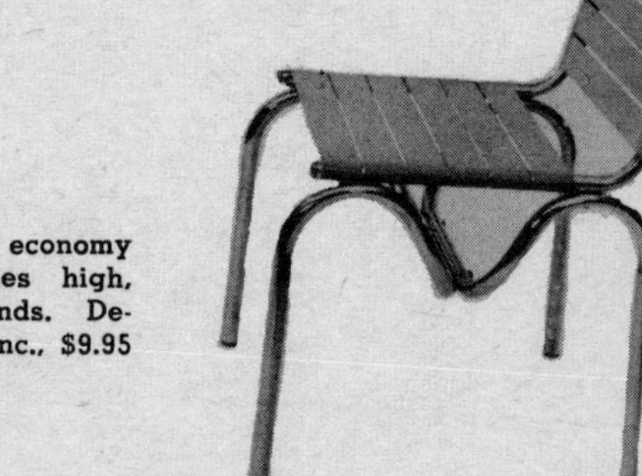

TABLE-HEIGHT economy chair is 34 inches high, weighs five pounds. Designed by Deeco Inc., $9.95

UTILITY BENCH with bright woven top can be used for serving as well as seating. It would also make a handy foot-rest. Manufactured by Kalamazoo $7.95

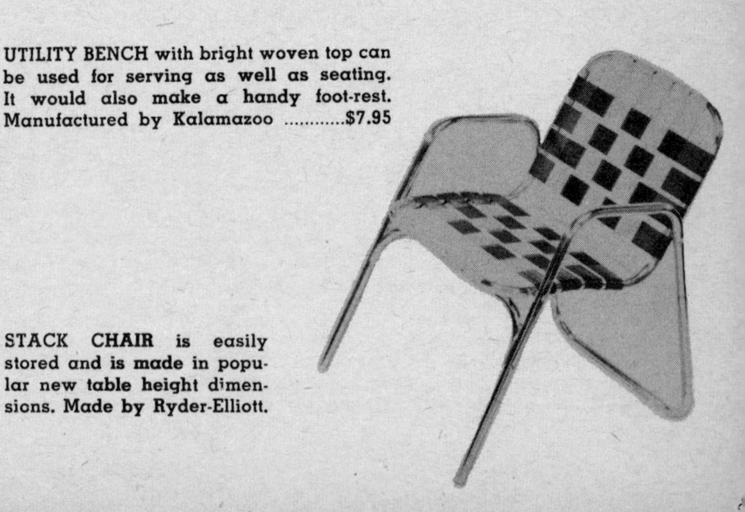

STACK CHAIR is easily stored and is made in popular new table height dimensions. Made by Ryder-Elliott.

THE CENTURIES-old beauty of Creole cast-iron furniture has now become universally available in cast aluminum. Use of this light metal results in radically lower shipping costs and brings the delivered cost within the reach of many more people. Moreover, pieces formerly cumbersome when cast in iron are light and portable when made of aluminum. •

RARELY SEEN traditional design in cast metal is "lily-of-the-valley." Indoor-Outdoor Shop $72.50

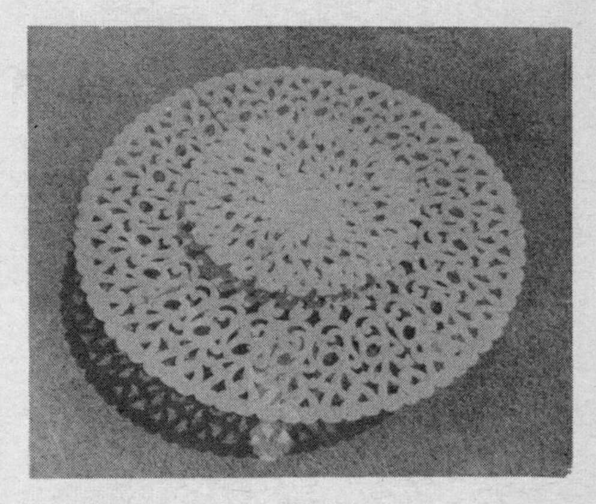

ROUND coffee table with Lazy Susan center is 42 inches in diameter. From Indoor-Outdoor Shop.

FORMAL NATCHEZ pattern is handsome in aluminum. Indoor-Outdoor: settee, $100; table, $39.50

ANCIENT FERN pattern gives flowing lines to settee, $100 and chair, $60, from Indoor-Outdoor.

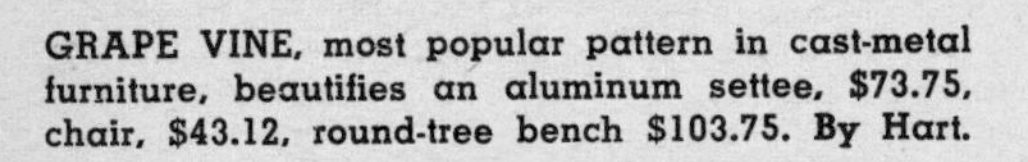

GRAPE VINE, most popular pattern in cast-metal furniture, beautifies an aluminum settee, $73.75, chair, $43.12, round-tree bench $103.75. By Hart.

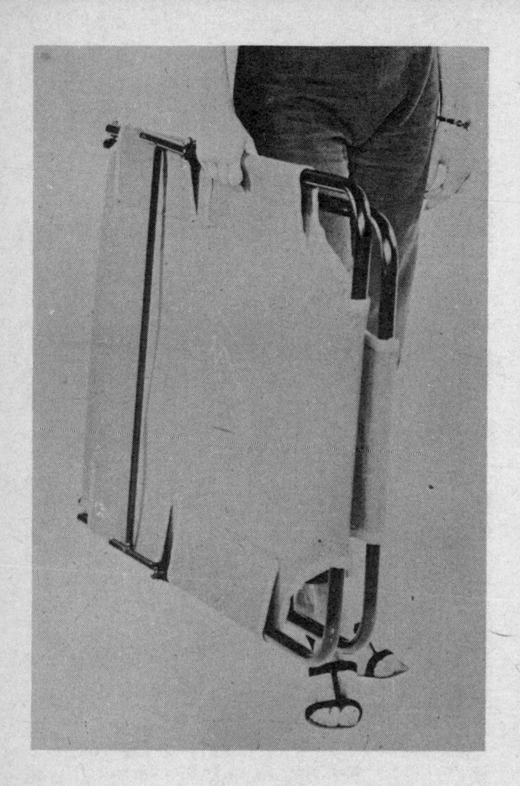

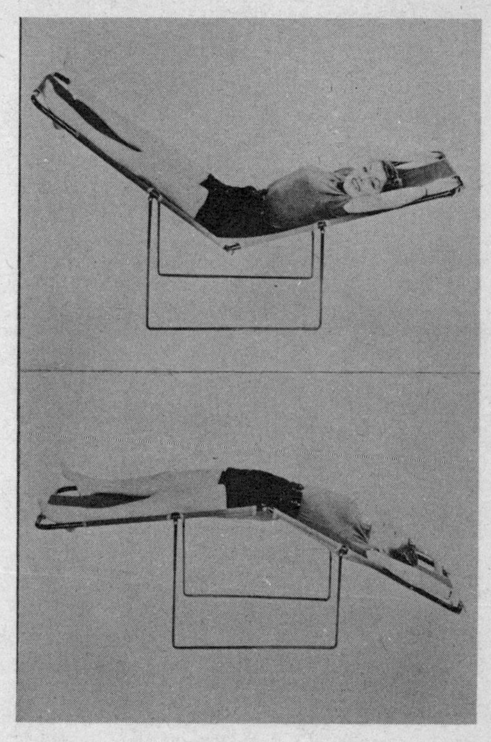

BRAND NEW patented idea in contour lounges is this Rx model in wrought iron and duck which folds into extremely portable package. May be used both as a lounge and an exerciser. By Inco Co., $29.95

ITALIAN MODERN school is represented by combination settee and umbrella table which make lavish use of expanded metal screening. Rust guarantee. John B. Salterini, 1 Park Ave., NYC.

TRADITIONAL and modern materials are elegantly combined in furniture of wrought iron and cast aluminum by Molla, Inc. Card table is $120; chair, $65; chaise, $175; nest of tables, $88

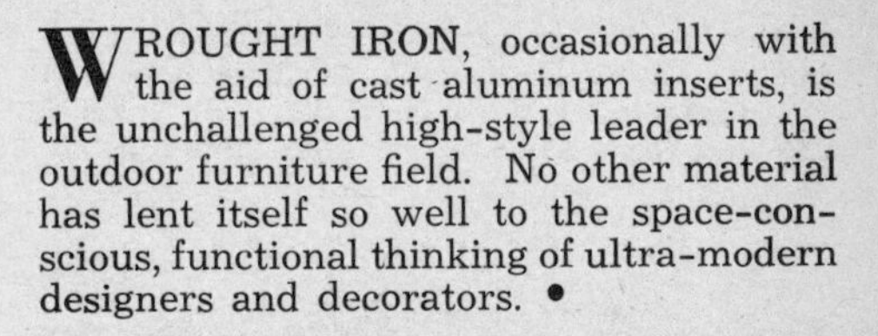

WROUGHT IRON, occasionally with the aid of cast aluminum inserts, is the unchallenged high-style leader in the outdoor furniture field. No other material has lent itself so well to the space-conscious, functional thinking of ultra-modern designers and decorators. •

NEW ENTRY in the indoor-outdoor field is San Souci casual chair. Duck, available in nine colors, is laced with braided orlon and may be easily removed for washing. Made by Gold Star Manufacturing Co., chair sells for $10.50

WOVEN WIRE basket is feature of new Sculptura design. This chair, manufactured by Lee L. Woodard Sons, is light, easy to move and can be left outdoors in any weather without damage.

HANDSOME GROUPS shown in two photographs above demonstrate exquisite designs available in wrought iron. They are just as suitable for indoor as for outdoor use. Lee L. Woodard Sons.

WARM TONES of rattan and redwood are emphasized by gold-anodized aluminum frames in this beautiful, light-weight dining set. Table is $55 and chair $31 from the Troy Sunshade Co.

RATTAN furniture creates warm tropical atmosphere, is light in weight, sturdily built and very durable. The armchair is $33 and the three-piece sectional priced at $80 from Tropical Sun Co.

TRAY table is $22.50; chair, $21.50, by Tropical.

ROUND table by Tropical is $14; armchair, $21.50

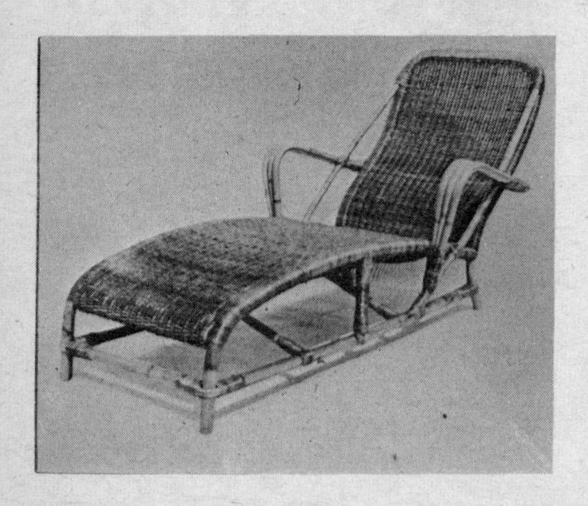

RATTAN CHAISE by Tropical is priced at $60

FISH-SHAPED chaise by Tropical is priced at $60

CONTEMPORARY cone and sunburst chairs combine imported rattan with black tubular steel or gold-anodized aluminum. By Troy Sunshade, $29

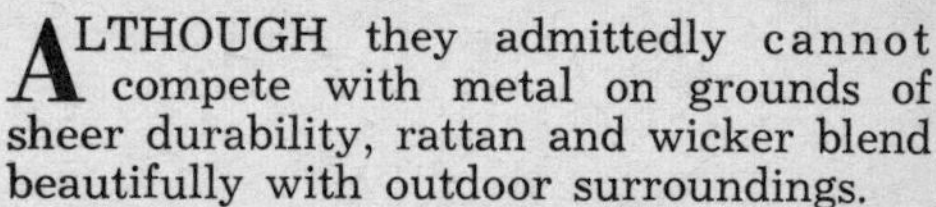

ALTHOUGH they admittedly cannot compete with metal on grounds of sheer durability, rattan and wicker blend beautifully with outdoor surroundings.

For indoor-outdoor use, where furniture is not intended to be constantly exposed to the weather, these materials are rapidly increasing in popularity. They tend to bring a feeling of the outdoors into the home, and are smartly styled. •

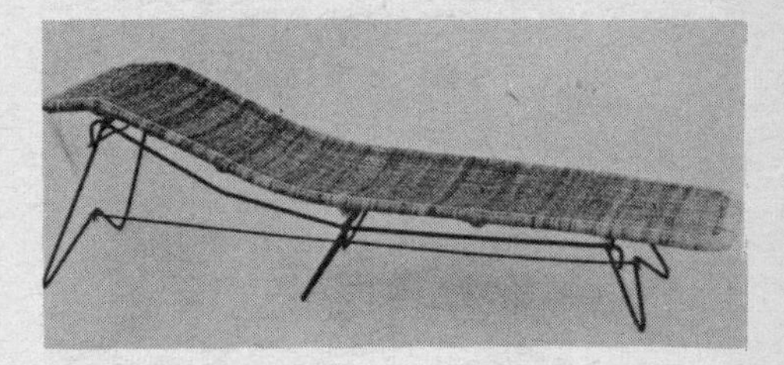

MUCH of the furniture shown on these two pages features Palembang, an oriental wicker with a rich golden color. The daybed at right, which costs $45, and the group below is by Tropical Sun.

SNACK table costs $30; stool, $5.80; chair, $30

COFFEE table is $20; chair, $19.70; ottoman, $12

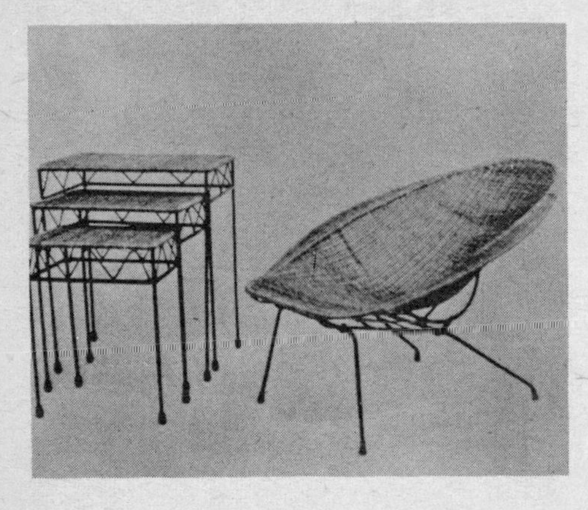

SHELL CHAIR is $25, nest of tables costs $30

BAR STOOL is priced at $13.50; planter, $18.50

BUDGET-PRICED director's chair has sculptured lines, latest plastic fabric, steel hardware. By Telescope Folding Furniture Co., it costs $6

WELL-MADE captain's chair in redwood is assembled with rustproof cadmium-plated bolts and screws. By Nason's Outdoor Furniture, it is $11.50

LOUNGE chair with canopy typifies trend toward brighter, more weather-resistant materials and better framework contours. Made by Telescope, it costs $11.40 with the canopy, $9.40 without.

GIN-RUMMY set of redwood has reinforced aluminum-strap base with spring suspension. Table has hole and rack for umbrella. Made by Nason's Outdoor Furniture, it costs $59.50 with pads.

WOODEN furniture, the original outdoor favorite, is still high in popularity because of its durability, its low price and its appropriateness to outdoor settings.

Recently traditional folding wooden furniture has undergone big changes. Parts that once were no more than square-cornered, barely-finished sections of lumber are now gracefully rounded and tapered, carefully sanded and varnished. Use of the latest plastic fabrics adds to the look of quality.

The perennial standby, redwood outdoor furniture, also continues to hold its own. •

NEW LOOK in wooden folding chairs features tapered, well-finished lines. Deluxe director's chair by Telescope has brass hardware, is $11.50

RUSTIC WHITE cedar patio sectional has the most rugged possible construction, moderate price. The entire group, by Brill Mfg., costs $99.50

REDWOOD Bench-table unit is sturdy, untippable, made to last for years. Manufactured by Nason's Outdoor Furniture, complete unit costs $31.50. Makes a fine dining table for back-yard picnics.

CLEAN LINES, legs of square iron tubing, padding suit this redwood set to indoor-outdoor use. By Nason's Outdoor Furniture, chaise is $47.50, settee $55, chair $41, cocktail table $24.50

NEW ALUMINUM umbrella permits adjustment to any tilt angle by rotation of umbrella's edge. Made by Crown Venetian Blind, it costs $99.95. Note elimination of usual scallops from design.

EVEN the garden umbrella is in a state of constant evolution and improvement. Simpler methods of raising and lowering, easier methods of adjusting their angle of tilt, have had the special attention of manufacturers recently. Scallops on aluminum umbrellas and fringes on those covered with fabric are beginning to disappear from many lines. The brighter-color fashion has taken over in the umbrella field, too, even to the use of anodized-aluminum finishes. Two-layer plastic fabrics, solid-colored on the outside and with gay floral prints on the inside, are becoming increasingly popular. •

INGENIOUS new pull-cord adjustment eliminates all the work of raising and lowering umbrella. Even a child can operate it. These models with fringed scallops are by the Macon Umbrella Corp.

DISTINCTIVE palembang umbrella-table set has contemporary form, blends with outdoor surroundings. Observe how umbrella filters sunlight. From Tropical Sun, table is $30, umbrella $98

AMAZING new mechanism for raising, lowering and tilting is completely concealed inside pole, effortlessly operated by small hand crank. Deluxe trim has vinyl exterior and chintz lining. Prices start at about $50 from Troy Sunshade Co.